SOCIAL ENGINEERING
THEORY AND PRACTICE

Exposing the reality of Government
manipulating their citizens

Mark R. Blum

Dedicated to the hundreds of millions of human victims.

The political dissidents and innocent people murdered
by the blood-soaked hands of their own governments:
Killed and or abused because of intolerance for a diversity of opinions.
In the former Soviet Union; Communist China;
Nazi Germany; Cambodia and elsewhere in
the world; to name but a few examples;
particularly the innocent children.

May mutual respect
free speech and freedom of conscience
always reign supreme.

HARBINGER
Consultants Incorporated

Mr. Mark R. Blum

ORDERING INFORMATION:

Quantity sales: Special discounts are available on quantity purchases by corporations, associations, and others. For details, contact: Kindle | Amazon.com or the author. Orders by trade bookstores and wholesalers.

Publisher's Cataloguing-in-Publication Data:
Blum, Mark R. | Social Engineering Theory and Practice . Exposing the reality of Government's manipulating their citizens. | Mark Richard Blum.

ISBN:
Paper Back Copy: 978-1-7751695-3-6
E-book copy: 978-1-7751695-2-9

The main category of the book: Social Engineering | Philosophy | Humanities | Psychology.
Subject category: Social Engineering | Commentary and analysis concerning the political, and social practice of human behavioural engineering | Manipulation of human behaviours | Mark Richard Blum.

Title: Social Engineering Theory and Practice.

Cover Design / Graphic Artist: Nuha Smith

First Edition

CONTENTS

INTRODUCTION

Chapter 1

Perspective

Social Engineering Theory & Practicalities

Chapter 6

Mind Over Human Nature

Introduction

SOCIAL ENGINEERING THEORY AND PRACTICE is a topic every human being needs to understand because like it or not, Social engineering is a reality in how we are governed. Every law and activity of Government alters society. Those who influence society via advertising, political action or ideas in and of themselves encompasses Social engineering; and no one alive in contemporary society can escape its over powering influence. It is prudent to acquire an understanding and perspective of how we are all manipulated in our personal and public lives. It is my desire as the author via this book to explain the effects of Social engineering in contemporary society and create a set of standards to be applied in the practice of what I consider "ethical", Social engineering Theory and Practice. I have been aware of this all my life; -*now I want to inform you, how your being played with for other people's purposes.*

WHERE DID THIS PRACTICE ORIGINATE?

Social engineering is a term that references the covert manner society is manipulated and explains its effects upon our social condition; regardless if we are aware of it or not. Since the end of WWII, western societies have intensified their Social engineering practices. These initiatives under the Prussian educational model, where initially invoked *via Government in the modern context within our children's schools. This program starts* with military regimentation of all students to form lines; followed by roll call; and then the national anthem. In the class room we find controlled speech (raise your hand); controlled activities (follow the teachers orders); controlled curriculum (determined by the Government) and provides the agenda of the curriculum which edits information for purposes of indoctrination (controlled perspectives). All independence is denied in favour of regimentation and the requirement for seeking permission to do anything, to create an environment of submission to authority. Social engineering got its modern-day start intending to instil discipline in Prussian children for future military service. There is a correlation between military discipline and school discipline by intentional design. This book explains many other aspects of Social engineering that most citizens in Western nations take for granted and due to lack of understanding we fail to realize, we are all being and have been manipulated from kindergarten to graduation, to serve Government or other people's purposes. Pragmatically to be an employee of the industrial machine and follow orders, thus other people's agendas.

I seek to define Social engineering in its scope of activities and intentional implementations. To explain, where and how it takes place, how we are all being manipulated our entire lives; and your life has been hijacked; Social engineering takes many forms. This stoic philosophic book looks at what is Social engineering and reveals how it has often been implemented with good intentions and catastrophic results in our day to day lives. That too much social manipulation takes place by vested interests in the form of laws, corporate
agendas and other social constructs in society today; without considering the long-term often detrimental outcome of these policies and manipulations.

My intention is to reform and refine Social engineering, to create a body of perspective which considers authentic human nature. Social engineering as it is currently practiced is an ad-hock social manipulation and construct. The effects of a lot of Social engineering have harmed society, by not considering the long-term consequences of these laws. Social engineering Theory and Practice was written from the perspective that Social engineering has been employed by those in power since the dawn of history, thus by creating a new doctrine that is pragmatic; I hope to reform this practice and its implementation. This book is a candid assessment of how to repair society; in societies' best interest. Intended to create an awareness that how we manipulate our society with laws and propaganda that needs to follow a structure of careful analysis, and professional awareness, that laws and policy have consequences, and require perspective. Like it or not; Social engineering is a fact of life and here to stay.

MY BACKGROUND

It is said that the parents mould the child, and as I reflect upon my childhood, I have at this late age started to reflect in recent decades regarding the effects of my own childhood. My father has had a profound influence upon my thinking, most likely because he was a profound person. I come from a mixed heritage as do most Canadians in this, Heinz 57 nation of peoples whose family have lived in this country for any length of time. Both of my parents have had a strong influence, but my father's influence has more to do with this book. My father was of mixed German heritage raised in Germany during the second world war and fortunately for him, he was a child; perhaps unfortunately. Because of the many hardships and traumatic experiences my father lived through. I learnt about the murder of half our family in the camps; followed by the gang raping of his mother by Russian occupiers at the end of the war. Both my father and his sister are the only Blum's to have survive the war; that we know of; thus, I grew up without paternal ancestors; other than my father's mother. When I was a child, we used to say our father had a "bad temper". Now years later I realize he suffered from severe post traumatic stress disorder. My brothers and I knew that it was better we did not step out of line when Dad was home.

Progressing into my teen years, my parent's deficiencies moderated, and our relationship changed. I would have many conversations with my father about current affairs and politics and could see that in addition to being a very conservative man, my father was also very skeptical about Government, politics, politicians and most people. My father's common expression when referring to certain politicians was to call them; "clowns". He did not mean this in a conventional pejorative sense, as I came to understand his use of the term. I believe he meant that they had no concept regarding the implications of their actions. My father I later came to realize saw the duplicity of politics and society as he was raised initially in the Nazi state and saw half his family murdered by that state in the concentration camps as they, to quote my German Grandmother; "Disappeared". My father had another favorite expression where he would call certain perspectives; "Brainwashing" which was his term for social indoctrination. It must be referenced that my father received the standard Nazi doctrinal education, then after the war still being a child; he was re-educated that everything he was told was truth during his formative years as a child was a lie. Clearly the contradictions would cause any thinking person to become skeptical about everything. Because of his skepticism my father taught me the importance to "think for myself" and thus after years of such healthy skepticism, I have come to have a different perspective.

Thus, I received as a child a healthy dose of cynicism from my father about everything. I learnt to think outside the box and think for myself as a child, where we stayed out of our father's way. Mother would advise us children, as was common in those days to: "get out of the house and play outside". Basically, my brothers and I were raised as feral weeds in a field: it has taken me decades to figure out why. I was, I now realize, my father's favorite; as my brother's accurately accused me. Dad and I could relate concerning his intellectual interests, and sometimes we would even share books we would read together each taking turns using the same book; *we became very close.* My father was my earliest tutor of politics, history and philosophy, he was an intellectual man. I recall his Christmas present each year being a book, in fact giving each other books at Christmas was a family tradition. I remember my father spent his holidays and weekends reading. I recall him reading Darwin's Origin of the Species which he got for Christmas one year and Immanuel Kant, books which he introduced to me also. I remember my Dad reading in his bedroom, spending hours alone; he always had two books by his side; - one the book he was reading, and the second a German-English dictionary. He never spoke or encouraged his children to speak German or have any connection to things German, he put the past behind him and his family; - at least he tried.

Talking about Germany, or things German got his ire up; so, the topic was avoided. We would debate; Mom called it; "arguing"; and I must say more than a few times he would leave the table in anger because my counter argument was not to his liking. Frequently Dad and I on a Saturday morning would go downtown, to the many used bookstores that existed at that time to browse for and buy books. Through my teen years, philosophical conversations at the dinner table; were a regular topic. These early childhood memories spawned the man I would become. The intellectual interests I present in my books; and my perspective on life. It has taken me three decades of reflection to realize the profound influence that years of those conversations with Dad would have on my life. My favorite place at high school was the school library, where I would check out books every other day; I was a veracious reader and had a large personal library to match.

MY MISSION

Thus, I have for my lifetime been on a personal mission to provide a stoic examination of life as it exists pragmatically. To figure out what is wrong with the world and society, to answer the questions of why life is like this, and how I can devise a strategy to improve this world to be a better place. Because of my father's influence and our intellectual connection, I have had a profound interest in how society functions and what makes society tick for as long as I can remember. Thanks to my father's tutelage, I have spent a lot of time reading about philosophy, politics, business and human psychology. I have come to recognize that much of the system is soiled by corruption. I see this as my life time project to change societies perspective from its current nihilistic projection to a more conscious and aware perspective. Other people have frequently referred to me as: "an agent of change," "a creative person" and "an idealist". My point of view has become backed up by my pragmatic perspective based upon my personal business and work experience. I believe I am pragmatically qualified in that I have on the ground experience concerning how the world "Really functions."

I have been writing for my entire life about social matters which interest me. I have taken it upon myself to research for many decades and mould my ideas from my reading and life experience with the healthy skepticism I acquired as a child.

The American philosophical school of thought called "pragmatism." has grown to become the central theme of my perspectives. One of my all-time favorite books has been Ralph Waldo Emmerson's; "Essay on Self Reliance." and Henry David Thoreau's book; "Walden", and the Mediations by Marcus Aurelius I have long been focused upon uncovering problems and the possible solutions to those issues. I have determined to speculate on the methodologies that could resolve many of societies ills. When in my youth I thought I would wait until I grew older and had more life experience to seek publication, to ensure my perspective is based upon enough experience, to be able to present my views based upon pragmatism not simply theory; but with an awareness of how the world functions in reality.

THE LACK OF PUBLIC AWARENESS

I have been very pleasantly surprised to discover that though there is a lot of public commentary concerning Social engineering in public debate; there is very little written on the topic specifically. There are no definitive works in this field of study regarding social engineering currently in print, based upon my research. There are books looking at social engineering from a perspective of internet use; but none as I refer to the terminology which is its original definition. Thought Social engineering is widely practiced, its refinement as a field of endeavour has not been achieved. Social engineering has no real authorities espousing the field's proper implementation. The philosopher Bertrand Russell and Karl Popper have presented perspectives, though no authentic analysis of social engineering's outcomes, and little concerning the ethics of such social manipulation by government. The topic is seen as controversial, though I do not see it that way, as we are all engineered by our parents and then our education. It is my desire to create a conscious analysis of public Social engineering that creates a body of ethics in the exercise of Social engineering in practice. I believe that my ethically composed philosophy of Social engineering will remove the hazard of the practice; which I see as corrupted vested interest. We need as a society to stop bumbling in the way Governments create legislation and achieve a better understanding of the implications of social reform. We also need to become consciously aware that as citizens we are being manipulated by many forces with a vested interest; and that this is creating a great deal of undue social harm.

This topic has interested me my entire life. My desire is to remove the legislated political process of social engineering from ad-hoc implementation to a profession worthy of consultation. I desire to present the unvarnished truth about Social engineering and advise regarding its legitimization. To create a conscious discipline of Social   Engineers, by defining and refining its methods of operation and ethical instruments, by altering its perspective. From my perspective we need to:

1. Bring the field of Social   engineering into the twenty-first century, as a positive and progressive field of study.

2. We unfairly expect our politicians to be all knowing and trustworthy; this is opposed to the reality of human biological nature and weakness.

3. Those in authority usually, with few exceptions, become corrupted by vested interests instead of fiduciary integrity; as people in positions of power are pulled in different directions by various forms of seduction in exchange for commissions of a breach of trust; often by financial incentive, sometimes by intimidation, and by other forms of seduction. This appeal to human weakness avails itself from others who want to co-opt the power inherent in all positions of authority for personal or group gain. The seducers are a whole host of vested interests. Power corrupts, because power can create opportunity for others; because human beings are biologically easy to seduce due to our: needs, greed and egotistic weakness.

4. Human positions of authority must be tempered, by regulating the controller's authority; because humanity has a fundamental weakness in that with power comes seduction; towards our corrupt hearts, and the corrupt hearts of others; motivated by the desire for gain and egotism. Due to this foundation of human vulnerability when in positions of power it is my contention that; no person can be trusted with too much authority who suffers from human frailties (which we all have) to various forms of seduction. The desire and ability to co-opt authority is just too prevalent. Power corrupts, because human biological frailties are corruptible, and we all

have weakness for some form of temptation naturally, also human beings can be very duplicitous; especially in positions of power.

5. I intend to create processes and perspective regarding social policy that has an ethical compass to guide its practitioners. I hope this book will supply a piece of the foundation for the necessary social and political reformation. The proper implementation requires protection from corruption of the Social Engineers from creating false narratives due to corrupt processes. Corruption as in all instances of human malfeasance can only be prevented by the application of checks and balances within the system of regulation which is a part of the scope of this work. The expression, "Mexican stand off", comes to mind as how best to remedy human corruption in the design of political institutions in my perspective.

6. This book is not regulatory; but rather an exercise in assembling the pieces of our social puzzle to create perspective for reform. To encourage the engagement of social discourse and the utilization of the latest in human scientific, sociological and other knowledge, as we build our social structures cognitively. Rather than the ad-hoc impulsive practices of the past. The governance of humanity has thus far been the tale of brutality. We as a species need to evolve sufficiently to finally develop society consciously, and to behave as fiduciaries for our species. If we do not, then we are definitely doomed as our technology is quickly surpassing our sociological development, and will result in horrific egotistical tyranny, followed by self inflicted destruction of our civilization; as an obviously predictable outcome.

7. I feel the need to alert society that Social engineering is a reality and is often very negative in its ramifications when not properly implemented. This is a work of social political critique and social political reform.

8. Social engineering Theory and Practice is also a field guide and is meant to create a profession that conducts research and reports; utilizing scientific methodology and peer reviewed studies; that pre-analyzes; all

human history and implications for government policy this has created, determines validity of ideas based upon analysis of pragmatic outcomes across the spectrum of social sciences.

9. The Social Engineer needs to be aware of the methodology and intent of past Social engineering and the pragmatic outcome of legislation upon the human social evolutionary experience. The fundamental understanding of human psychology and particularly human nature is a foundation without which Social engineering becomes tyranny. Social Engineers must compose reports that are both ethical and un-tainted by bias, analysis of social factors and to project outcomes, based upon authentic human nature which the social engineer must have a clear grasp of.

10. I believe Social Engineers will one day be capable of creating an historically based predictive computer macro which will generate reports and projections that automatically create analysis. If historical data is broken down into cognitive bits of events and outcomes. There is a strong bases to believe that an algorithm may be created to conduct such predictive analysis. Once historical data and human nature has been defined as an assembly of pieces of historical and psychological fact, that can be brought forward. Such a computer algorithm would be based upon human history, and human nature which is stagnant and thus predictable in long term outcomes. Once humanity overcomes our governance problems in eliminating tyranny, I believe we can focus more upon the progressive development of civilization into the cosmos, which is our next stage in evolutionary development.

11. The Social Engineer must clearly comprehend human nature in terms of both our strengths and weaknesses. Must take a macro approach to comprehending and performing comprehensive social analysis.

12. To professionalize the field of Social engineering to be refined to have a cautious and a wholistic perspective; as this book defines these perspectives. Legislators re-

quire independent professional and scientific reviews supplied by analysis of current literature, from various studies and or vetted scientific research; that provides a depth of understanding regarding what they are voting in favor of or opposed to in terms of implementations and dominos that are set in motion by legislation. Clearly there is no tolerance for the unelected judiciary acting to exceed law enforcement and the creation of precedents I see as little more than dictatorial powers that have no value to an authentic democracy.

Our society is plagued with problems of bias and force being applied, and yet there is not a philosophy that ethically performs pre-analysis of societies problems pragmatically. There is no authentic unbiased definitive academic discipline of Social engineering. Perspective is essential to all political fields of endeavour; for without this we only serve to introduce piece meal, shallow policies, that cause a great deal of harm to society as presented by the examples in this book.

This brings about issues of moral relativism as I explain; there is no relativism as some people would suggest in argument. Social engineering ethics is explained herein as I provide a wholistic ethical perspective, as outlined to help guide the profession of Social Engineers. Human society must be stoically structured to reflect the natural character of humanity, for the benefit of society; not simply vested interests as is the current circumstance. My perspective is one of bringing forth individual liberty which comes with individual responsibility and is a perspective of Social engineering intended to alter society to encourage an attitude of self reliance that pragmatically enables, us all. And is true to human nature as I will explain.

HISTORY

Social engineering predates the computer, and also the internet. One definition of Social engineering commonly utilized at present cites Social engineering as limited to computer based social media. In reality Social engineering encompasses much more in the realm of manipulating individual and group social perspectives in society. Also, manipulating law, courts, Government policy, and business; due to a vested interest or political agenda. Social engineering is commonly implemented via presenting perspectives that have no foundation in research or comprehension of the long-term effects and implications of the concepts advocated and put forth:

1. A lot of present-day Social engineering utilizes un-vetted sociology, scientifically false narratives and perspectives, to benefit vested interest groups, without utilizing scientific methodologies to determine the universal validity of the concepts espoused.

2. Misrepresents the facts, in being derived from perceptions; suffers from a lack of vetted facts regarding a given policy to manipulate public opinions and perceptions intentionally via sleight of hand policies.

3. Utilizing invalid un-censored by scientific method, rudimentary information; that encompasses Social engineering in its negative application.

4. By taking advantage of the social character of people, and thus manipulating legal, commercial or political change via emotional manipulation without benefit of validated fact. Representative of vested interests, in contravention of having any authority to implement fundamental social change by overreaching legislation that has ramifications which over time manifest as detrimental to society.

5. Social legal change not being based upon validated knowledge or research which verifies the perspective or intended change. Social engineering can be both harmful and detrimental to a given society by imposing change that is regressive towards society's improvement and that is nihilistic; and thus, detrimental in its long-term impact imposed upon society.

6. Social engineering exceeds corruption, in that it has the nation state take on religious roles in enforcing personal

morality and ethics due to humanist political and or philosophical ideologies dominating the nation state in recent decades. It is in essence totalitarian government at its core. By its intention it seeks to control people's private lives by others. It is now practiced extensively in virtually every western nation and many others. Freedom in the west; as in free individual choice regarding your personal life has been crushed; as I will proceed to open your eyes further.

The trial of the Greek philosopher Socrates in ancient Athens is an example of society's resenting and wanting to shut down free thought as he was charged with corrupting the youth. This is a very ancient example of Social   engineering on the part of the Athenian state, by censoring the teachings of Socrates that taught his students to; question everything! The social controllers; those with vested interests in the state legally prosecuted Socrates in that infamous trial: De-indoctrination of the brainwashed, has long been a risky activity. Other early perspectives regarding Social   engineering include: The philosophical book; "The Open Society and its Enemies, Volume 1, The Spell of Plato". Written by the philosopher Sir Karl Raimund Popper who examined; "the application of critical and rational methods of science, to the problems of open society Vs. tribalism and the distinction of peace meal Social   engineering and utopian Social   engineering". Popper held that social affairs are unpredictable. He argued vehemently against Social   engineering utilizing the writings of Plato's Republic as an example Vs Socratic open society. He also sought to shift the focus of political philosophy away from questions about who ought to rule, toward questions about how to minimize the damage done by authorities which I concur with as necessary. In Chapter 3 / Notes 7-9, section of Popper's book; item 9; Popper supplies a history of the use of the term; "Social   engineering". I present this information here for your historical reference of the term; Social   engineering". Social   engineering is primarily Government interference and creeping interloping afflicting the private and personal civil lives of a nation's citizens. Traditionally such concepts have been the domain of personal religious beliefs, ideologies or utopian ideas, which fail to recognize the diversity of humanity in that: your utopia might be my nightmare. Political fanaticism is one of the most murderous attitudes in the history of humanity.

MASS MEDIA: RADIO & TELEVISION

The advent of the radio in Nazi Germany was the beginning of mass propaganda and manipulation of a nation's citizens as never observed in history. This era of mass broadcasting commenced authentic mass propaganda and social manipulation as never in history which was inserted into people's homes. This occurred in all western nations for the first time with the invention of the radio in the 1930s. The population having no sophisticated comprehension of what propaganda is; or perspective regarding this new media; took it at face value as some still do to this day, not realizing fake stories are sometimes planted to alter public opinions towards accepting a course of action; *even war!* The people were naïve and believed what they were told. The spirit of an independent news media as a meeting place for ideas carried over from newspapers and print journalism temporarily; in western nations relative freedom of media prior to the consolidation of media empires took place for about fifteen to twenty years after the end of the second world war. But as time has worn on, private and Government vested interest; sometimes being one and the same in the west, have taken over broadcast media. The fundamental problem with this is that as contradictions in reporting leak out, over time the media loses credibility, and thus, we get to the point we have today where in the media are increasingly seen as enemies of the people, in some social circles; *this is unprecedented!* Where in past decades people sought the news; now many turn it off in belief it is filled with lies. Media has become; rather than a reporting of what occurred they now engage in reporting what occurred in a highly edited fashion, followed by an editorial lecture presenting slanted points of view that makes no effort to pursue an alternative perspective (*called balanced reporting*); thus, it reveals its intention as being to indoctrinate. Nazi propaganda Minister Joseph Goebbels was the first to tout the effectiveness of the "Big lie". A lie so big as to be broadcast thus is unfathomable for society to conceive it is an absolute lie.

Communism, which advocates atheism, thus encounters an ethical dilemma and problem which is seldom addressed, and that is, the personal ethics of the individual. Thus, the logical extension of this, is that the nation state must thus become totalitarian to fulfill this role and become the new pope or priest of society by extension. In nineteen thirties Europe both communism and fascism acted as competing ideologies. This is the primary foundational source of Social engineering as both the fascists of Germany and the communists of the Soviet Union indoctrinated their citizens with ideologies. Interesting to note that both are currently failed states that no longer exist. Nazi Germany from war and intolerance that taught the world the dangers of racist national policies gone too far, in an era were worldwide racism was a reality. Communism seeing religion as the "opium of the masses;" to quote Karl Marx is an atheist state and by implication this ideology requires the state to interlope and regulate people's private lives. It infiltrates matters regulating citizens personal and private family affairs; and thus, de-facto removes the concept of a separation of church and state. This is the derivative of communist and Marxist theory, by extension this mandates hypocritical state interloping into the private religious morals and ethics of the nations' citizens. Thus, invading the private domain of citizens personal ethics and morals to become the newly created prerogative of the nation state. The area of a person's private life, which many people particularly in the west historically have considered to be their exclusive private domain; those matters in which many people would traditionally say is; *"personal"*, -or- *"none of the Government's business"*; the private individual's citizen's business has become Government business. This has resulted in further incursions; where free speech is now increasingly subjugated to state censorship in the west, as the nation state now becomes a surrogate God or like a Pseudo-Egyptian Pharos, with complete dominion over your entire life. Social engineering is when Government exceeds the mandate, to deal with and control what is traditionally called criminal acts and regulations of commerce. By Government creating laws that regulate personal matters of family, and that which was a traditional role of religion. This is where a lot of damaging Social engineering in one form or other as stated takes place. In that voluntary matters of traditional religious morals become laws of the nation state and are enforced by the state; i.e.: "Family law". In influencing individual behavior by Government initiatives and incentives built into economic policy and tax policy. Social engineering has been practiced for centuries; actions such as high levels of taxation called; "sin taxes" in many western nations on cigarettes, alcohol and drunk driving penalties etc. They added taxation to increase the price of purchase to the point that it reduces consumption. Not to mention the desire for the additional tax revenues this generates for the Government in a deceptive ploy. Commercial advertising is a form of Social engineering via indoctrination; that is intended to sway the consumer to acquire something for a benefit espoused by a corporation's message; or other social, political, or economic interest group.

Social engineering is primarily defined as encompassing Government supplementing religion to act with authority that even exceeds traditional religion, via its threat of violent enforcement, with a very ancient political and social intention; that being the establishments vested interest, over societies interests. It is in essence currently an authoritarian and totalitarian humanist counterfeit religion of the state, determining morality and enforcing it via the utilization of law-making authority. An example is state imposed de-facto marriage, known as "common law marriages" which are ("shot gun marriages") marriages imposed by the state, without consent required for the marriage *(the self-promoting business manifestations of the pearly mouthed judicial industry; know no boundaries)*. Thus, since the nineteen seventies common law marriage has become an imposed de-facto civil contract determined by Government. An oath of commitment freely and consciously entered into, voluntarily by the subject individuals is no longer required. Thus, common law marriage is an imposed marriage contract determined by Government. This has been followed by state-imposed child support laws and criminalization of private family relationship matters, such matters were traditionally requiring personal decisions and determinations. Creeping totalitarianism has been imposing itself as above individual liberty. This type of law-making is now imposed in most western nations and viciously enforced with legal ramifications imposed upon the individual, by the nation states interloping into private matters. Thus, voluntary collaboration via free will and civil contract; as is traditional marriage, has become a state sponsored dictatorial imposition that encompasses an extortion program; particularly for men. This also includes wide spread bigotry against paternal/shared child custody with new laws, wherein the bias in these cases has translated pragmatically into men losing all their parental rights and being diminished to the status of having "visitation privileges" regarding their own biological children. These extremely unequal bigoted laws, imposed by state sponsored sleight of hand, denying the biological and emotional reality of masculine child parent bonds, for political expediency by corrupt Government policies and legislation. The beneficiary of this is the judiciary themselves for their own vested financial interest; at the expense of children's rights. The Judicial industry receives annually tremendous financial reward in the Billions of dollars for perversely repressing masculine paternity and egalitarian legislation. The social consequence has been to impose a chilling effect upon child birth and family formation in western society. The result has been to create a social and individual trepidation towards both marriage and having children, as a direct result of the financial and emotional toll of these new Government policies, which came about due to the modification of divorce laws and the dishonourable judicial industry supplementing the contentious divorce with contentious child custody laws for their own financial benefit. Industrialization is often falsely cited as the cause of reduced childbirth in the west; this is not reality on the ground. There are two primary causes of the reduced child births in the west those being; economic inflation caused by mass feminine employment that has had an impact upon the cost of home ownership due to families having an increased income, and this severely impacting the ability of couples to be able to financially survive based upon one salary. This has made dual incomes financially necessary and handicapped western family's ability to care for children, with the Government cover story that this is due to feminism; which became a state financed Social engineering program, complete with designated Government Ministers. These nation states are now involved in population replacement, this has led to conspiracy theories that western Governments intentionally have destroyed all family incentive to justify bringing in passive workers to replace western workers who are too outspoken; on behalf of Government's corporate sponsors. Post war western prosperity only lasted during the first two decades after World War II, from the nineteen fifties to the nineteen seventies for the working class. After that period easy credit and revolving consumer debt has masked a general economic decline in the west. Where in a second family income moved from being a bonus to a necessity to survive due to inflation in the cost of everything and the extraction of western manufacturing resulting from corporate sponsored Government free trade agreements.

With their Social engineering and indoctrination programs, western Governments have made great strides in reconstituting the composition of families via Social engineering that encompasses legislated social change, that was gradually introduced strategically over several decades. They have thus removed the stigma of child illegitimacy, and the consequences of natural restrictions upon female reproduction due to the financial consequences of sexual promiscuity being removed under law. They also have removed voluntary male participation in child rearing; and replacing it with state sponsored extortion of males. While all reproductive authority, even birth termination has become exclusively the female domain, laws have been modified that exclude the male in all aspects of this determination, other than the requirement that males must fund a woman's decisions; without his consent being required. The principal of marriage contract; which has been traditionally a voluntary contract to raise children as a partnership, has been eroded in the social revolution against the very concept of family and partnership between both men and women. All of these changes in law and Government interloping have been short sighted and politically motivated vote getting activities of current politicians. These fundamental and foundational Government Social engineering initiatives were implemented without consideration for their long term deterministic social effects and outcome. There was never a wholistic consideration of the implications that the removal of personal responsibility would have; that in effect is the infantilization of both men and women by Government. Requiring male financial support of women, and men being stigmatized and pejoratively denigrated as incapable of child rearing; in contradiction to the past belief that paternalism was and is in reality the mother's choice and responsibility; except in cases of rape which is rare. However, in the case of a widower, such a pejorative anti-paternal attitude would be hypocritically be considered a social outrage. Historically, out of wedlock child birth was fundamentally the mother's determination exclusively as well as her financial responsibility as these rights of determining the child's fate were hers alone if not married, (under a contract of marriage) as were the obligations to support the child was hers alone. Because the state did not want to carry the financial liability for massive welfare funding this caused. Government shifted responsibility for the outcome of these laws upon men who now be-cry; "Foul".

Because of major changes in law permitting divorce, social customs and laws were Socially engineered by Governments in western nations in the nineteen sixties and seventies to make fathers liable financially for out of wed lock child births; this is outside the traditional common law customs of the west spanning millenniums. Once divorce creates child illegitimacy what should they do? They Socially engineered the legitimization of the illegitimate, then ensured the mother's rights of determining the child's fate and gave the father the financial liability with completely bigoted law preventing even joint custody with fathers, who are cast out and disposed of by these Social engineering laws. Contrary to claims of equal rights, that was the original premise of many pro-feminist and egalitarian laws that were long overdue in fairness. When it comes to child custody equality in these hypocritical nations with constitutions claiming everyone must be treated equally is a mass social fraud perpetrated by the judicial industry as the pragmatic reality is that men's biological connections and love for their children via permitting equal custody and access to children of divorce would be very financially costly in loss of business for the judicial industry also. Their systematic bigotry program is highly profitable for the legal establishment who needed some way to supplement their income post "no fault divorce legislation" That has seen this industry grow exponentially in practitioners and profits; judicial corruption is rampant! This is a prime example of vested interest imposing Social engineering for their own profit and illustrative of how Social engineering by the elite is used to extort money from the working class who can ill afford this social   structure and thus western nations now have extinction birth-rates.

Social engineering is also now practiced to silence Government opposition by increasingly legislating the legal imposition of what is called; "politically correct speech". This has served to shield the modification and the reduction of political opposition to Social engineering. These recent developments demonstrate a trend away from scientifically based analysis of the social effects of new laws prior to their implementation; without such pre-analysis and studies encompassing psychological research into human nature these developments have been very damaging to western society as speech repression is an increasing phenomenon in western nations. Because Government have become increasingly interventionist thus interloping via Social   engineering the west has become increasingly totalitarian. Marriage is no longer a prerequisite for child bearing and trust between men and women has been eroded to the point where in western child reproduction has reached extinction levels and geriatric majorities of the domestic population are growing. This now requires mass immigration to supplement the population, causing conflict over fundamental cultural change. Large scale immigration initiated thus is creating a cultural clash that is an increasing problem instigated by Government policies of multiculturalism, versus the traditional and historical melting pot perspective regarding immigrants. This creates as a result a formula where in immigrants are increasingly being seen as foreign rather than new members being welcomed into western societies. This fundamental social   change is the source of increasing social   friction and social   divides. The net effect is similar to a colonial conquest in altering the fundamental acceptance of immigration as a result. The domestic population perceive, and in fact are experiencing Government policies of affirmative action towards immigrants that diminishes their opportunities in Government and private sector employment. Thus, the population of these nations are increasingly feeling justifiably betrayed by their Government(s) in this additional way, as a result of these intended legislated Social engineering policies in the treatment of immigrants by granting privileges that sometimes exceed those of the domestic population. Meanwhile the core of the nation's existing population and founding peoples, are displaced by what are called "paper citizens;" -born elsewhere. None of these Social engineering policies as revolutionary as they are regarding the personal lives of citizens was ever implemented via popular consent with a plebiscite. These policies constitute fundamental social change and are in reality beyond the scope of what is normal legislation; as they affect people so personally and impose ethical concepts upon the nation state's people that is semi religious in scope.

Given the populations preoccupation with the extraction of so much of their wealth in mortgages, that carry usurious interest amounts to be paid, and the heavy tax burden the middle class is weighed down with the requirement to work, more than ever by both spouses being required to work. This servitude by design of debt indenture, avails no time for protest, in order to survive. Excessively busy citizens are both hostile and complicit citizens, to Government manipulation. Western nations are some of the unhappiest nations on earth, as a result of all the stress this has caused society.

These very dangerous Government trends accounts for the current rise in populist nationalist government in the west, a growing level of racist attitudes and social resentment. This is potentially a very dangerous development that is destabilizing virtually every western nation at present; as it is contrary to the purpose of the nation state; that being the protection and favouritism towards the nation's founding people. Thus, there is a domino effect of low birth rates in the west, created by irresponsible and near-sighted Social engineering; in that it is ultimately destabilizing not only the family, but also the Government, and ultimately the ruling class itself. These are long-term results of improperly motivated Social engineering, performed for vested interest and political reasons. Thus, Governments are becoming increasingly draconian in an attempt to quell the resulting social unrest. Increasingly draconian laws, censorship, and repressive tactics are being implemented by Government; who in effect are the authors of their own demise historically, implicated by the fact that these developments are the result of their legislations' long-term effects. Demonstrating that proper analysis of such policies must be performed in the future, not to manipulate the population, but rather to in reality represent societies best interest; rather than those with a vested interest in manipulating public policy for their own financial benefit.

THE FRANKFURT SCHOOL

The neo-communist think tank known as "The Frankfurt School" was composed of intellectual communists who were refugees from Nazi Germany. This philosophical school of thought pursued what they call, "critical theory" this is also referred to as cultural Marxism. This is the source of the "politically correct speech" phenomenon in western societies. This restricts speech with the intention to not offend and is basically a surrogate for what has traditionally been called; Bad manners, being rude or disrespectful of others. Increasingly politically correct speech is becoming legislated speech limits by Government and now leading to compelled speech by Government legislation. What is being referred to here, is cited to be the bases of what is called the current, "western cultural war", which is a backlash to the censorship these legal restrictions have evoked upon western society.

Critical Theory was developed by The Frankfurt School's Max Horkheimer a neo-Marxist professor. Their membership's academic activities encompassed adulteration of ideas in the social sciences. They are seen to have contaminated academic fields of study in the bubble of academia, so as to overlay their theoretical concepts upon all fields of study in the humanities with concepts which supplement critical thinking, with amongst other concepts the idea of "repressed individuals and repressor individuals". Ideologies such as the concept of a "patriarchy" and "white privilege"; controlling society. By teaching social   concepts without benefit of scientifically based, and properly vetted research. Introducing their developed philosophical concepts in keeping with their social Marxist ideology added to the curriculum in many western universities. This infiltration and subversion of the studies in the humanities started in the nineteen forties with the arrival of this group of fleeing Communist academics and spread over the ensuing decades to become the curriculum of university humanities education at this time.

This is now called "postmodern critical theory" and politicizes social perceptions without factual bases by immigrant minorities who by virtue of being new arrivals (immigrants) and other young students too uneducated to realize the biased historical narrative of western civilization they are being taught. This fabricated historical and cultural narrative is being taught by communistic university professors. This type of education divides society into "oppressors and the oppressed" based upon race, and villainies placed upon the "white skin male" as the oppressor or "privileged beneficiary of society." The entire edifice of this subversive ideology is presented outside of any authentic historical narrative context; with regards to the historical realities of the white working class. Europeans founded western society hundreds of years prior and created the society immigrants and their families immigrated to. These founders are being criticised for their success, often by immigrants and their children who have left their own failed societies. These University students overlook the reality that the working class have had to protest and fight via unions and other measures in history to obtain the higher wages and benefits western society benefits from. All people in western societies are in fact privileged to be able to jump upon the coat tails of the hard work, and efforts of the very people who, have the birth right to enjoy a higher standard of living as inheritors of the benefits derived from their ancestors struggles and social battles. These same individuals who by virtue of being able to attend University are in their late teens and early twenties, lack the life experience and accurate historical narrative being supplied by their professors (who are the true villains here). Institutions that repeated surveys of academia have verified are filled primarily with idealistic communists, who never left the academic world, and thus have a distorted perspective on reality that lacks any pragmatic real-world experience. This is an explanation of the source of the Social engineering now being foisted upon the youth in most western nations at present which is a breach of trust by academia performed upon the youth. Instead of University being a source of education in critical thinking, they have become indoctrination camps, which cheat the youth of a proper education via focusing upon indoctrination rather than opening their minds to different perspectives and the value of independent thought as is the western educational tradition.

∞∞∞

NEGATIVE SIDE OF SOME SOCIAL ENGINEERING:
The implementation and use of manipulative practices to present a false narrative or opinion is one side of Social engineering which is very negative and has all too often been implemented. This type of policy does not follow a properly balanced, researched, vetted or understood via scientific determination of laws social impacts. Does not utilize scientific method to comprehend or empathize the cause and effect of certain conditions. Due to a lack of empathetic compassion and humanity in their approach and perspective tainted by

political correctness. Government interference into the personal and private lives of citizens has become rampant in western nations. This has led to laws and rules that have become totalitarian in the regulation of civil life. The nation state has become an enforcer of ethics called "Family Law", has created tyrannical civil law enforcement that has destroyed the motivation to have children or form families. Everything comes and goes in cycles, and I feel that keeping this in mind is a healthy stoic perspective; there will be repercussions for this tyranny that have yet to come to fruition first.

In seventeenth century America it was often said that; "Government is best which governs least". This is in recognition that laws with negative impacts often are enacted by Government without sufficient analysis and forethought of the impact upon society. The danger of a law that does not go through comprehensive vetting is the impact they can have to alter or change human behaviour. In my prior book; "The Libertarian Charter, how to get control of Government or it will control you". I present some of the impacts Government legislation has had upon current society. This book is intended to address the issue at the very core of these problems which are created by not vetting law making and enforcement decisions by Governments in recent years that are harmful acts which result in poor Social engineering practices with to a lesser degree good intentions. Law and law enforcement follow the old Christian expression of Jesus Christ and what is quoted as his last words to God; "Father forgive them, for they do not know what they do".

Nazi Germany's ideologies that lead to Governmental systematic extermination of those the regime perceived as of lesser quality. The utilization of a system of Gulags, and psychiatric institutionalization of political dissidents, in the former Soviet Union; for their perspectives that ran counter to the communist regime. Also, the Canadian Government's policy of kidnapping Native American children up until the nineteen nineties and placing them in brutal re-education schools to "take the Indian out of them", are several commonly understood examples of negative Social   engineering. The Eugenics movement of involuntarily sterilizing of the mentally handicapped and lobotomizing patients across north America, along with forced electro shock treatment and drug therapies in an attempt to induce behavioural modification of natural genetic variations in human populations from a perspective of having a moral or ethical superiority over those abused are clear examples of negative and thus harmful Social   engineering attempts. That if studied demonstrate how destructive to society and individuals such actions can be by unintended consequences or intention, that is often covertly malice based.

THE POSITIVE SIDE OF SOME SOCIAL   ENGINEERING:
Though social   engineering can sometimes lead to authentic political, social   reform and positive outcomes for the human condition which do not create social   discord. Positive Social   engineering in which the scientific method of vetting and confirmation via pragmatic testing is utilized; where sociological vetting takes place; where in research and literature is considered, in order to manipulate individuals and often society at large can be beneficial and is normally accepted by social   acquiescence. Examples of this are seat belt legislation requiring their use in vehicles, and feminist ideas of equal opportunity and treatment of both men and women. Also, removing Government legislated gender and racial restrictions, to have opportunities available to all people based upon a system of meritocracy; removing preconceived notions of class-based superiority that restricts opportunity; without the need for affirmative action which creates a synthesis of resentment and removes the principal of meritocracy. Sometimes good ideas go too far as moderation is necessary; something government commonly lacks.

Too often public policy in civil law is created in reliance upon un-egalitarian provision of opportunity without being merit based and becomes convoluting due to undemocratic often vindictive intentions without consideration for the social alienation and discord such actions create; and without compassion for those persons directly affected in a negative way by diminishing sociological reality for economic advancement, hindering those most qualified for opportunities. This is a repressive social policy, over perceived ability of the recipients of opportunity, thus creating social discord as the opportunities are thus perceived to be no longer merit based; but rather a variation of vindictive reverse discrimination. Emotion based reactions and Government policy without a foundation in utilizing a vetted science based conclusion or correctly implemented in reaction to holistic study of the cause, effect, and both long and short term outcomes generated by policy decisions and concepts, that upon the surface often look like good ideas; but which result in detrimental and or harmful long term effects by belittling the merit based ability of the recipient of such benefit; often create political and social instability. Seat of the pants policy implementation by Legislation, Government policy or business can and has often been very detrimental to society. Repressive actions are like insults in a debate, they only serve to provoke and prove the lack of validity of the reform implemented in order to silence criticism. Personal insult and politically correct speech is the instrument of weak perspectives and demonstrative of unfounded condescending arrogance. Negative Social engineering can be seen as politically correct speech which is intended to limit bigotry and control public discourse and are examples of that which becomes political repression of opinions which are unpopular with some segments of society who are usually beneficiaries. The prerogative of Social engineering can be either the veiled manipulation of people's options and perspectives; or policy based upon open consent which is superior in that it leads to the preferred social response of acquiescence. Social engineering often goes forth as public, group or business truisms' that lack vetted scientific study or other research and or academic evidence that validates the perspective being presented. All law causes social change that is often unexpected or even undesirable as an outcome.

VESTED INTEREST IN THE ESTABLISHMENT
Modern Social engineering commenced with the Prussian governmental political implementation of education reform to serve the military's purposes; various social policies such as universal health care, pensions and the encouragement of the production and eating of potatoes by the nation's population with an outcome intended to be of benefit to society, (sometimes un-vetted policy can be positive; though it is risky). Including the funding of Hegel to create a political philosophy that in effect advocating a totalitarian monarchy with what he called dialectic ideas. Much like Plato's advocation for "philosopher kings" in his case to unrealistically attempt to arrest political change, as he came from an establishment family and mourned their loss of political office, and perhaps his own political fantasies. Then there is of course Machiavelli who advocated all kinds of underhanded political practices in his well-known book "The Prince". Vested interest comes in many forms.

WHAT IS THE STUDY OF SOCIAL ENGINEERING?
The study of Social engineering is the review of attempts to manipulate the nature of the human being. Social engineering as it has been practiced in the past has been focused upon manipulating people for various purposes that are not their own as individuals, but rather for the gain or advantage of other persons or organizations. Like a scale, the balance of society changes with every law and Government policy. Religion, Government, Business and other organizations since the beginning of time have for centuries engaged in Social engineering of their people to solidify their positions of authority and to ensure the cooperation of citizenry. Sometimes with detrimental effects to society that were unforeseen, and which lead to causing violence and social discord; often resulting in violent

revolution.

TOOLS OF THE SOCIAL ENGINEER

The tools currently utilized in Social engineering are; Indoctrination, propaganda, false narratives, emotional manipulation, false and misleading information, acts of criminality, threats of violence, veiled and overt threats of prosecution and or imprisonment, intimidation through using the brute force of the state. Collusion and bribery, nepotism and favouritism towards groups in divide and conquer political strategy. While these techniques are all in existence as options to use there is a preference for those in power to avoid blunt instruments such as the unnecessary use of force unless as a last resort and when dealing with a reactionary who will queue jump to the use of force. Therefore, I have written this book with the desire to rectify the current situation and bring forth a basket of legitimate tools to correct the current corruption of social engineering and change this perspective. The foundations of the west are those of Socratic enquiry there is only one other option and that is authoritarianism which always leads to eventual collapse, as it becomes corrupted due to its illegitimacy via lacking acquiescence especially it leads to an eventual departure from pragmatic reality, due to detachment from the populous.

THE USE OF BRUTE FORCE AND VIOLENCE

Historically the prudent state does not want its brutal side to be exposed as for example it was demonstrated in the former eastern bloc of communist Europe. The rational being that if the silent majority turn against the state apparatus, the establishment loses it's co-opting the military and police, thus without these forces as in the collapse of the eastern bloc countries of Europe; then the entire state apparatus collapses. Once the credibility of the state is lost, the nation state lives upon borrowed time as revolt will result unless it can restore confidence. Such transformation can happen in as much as years or even hours as history has revealed. The nation state exists based upon its credibility. Government has always been about having credibility to ensure universal acquiescence. If you study sea farers of the past four or five hundred years you soon realize that without the greater state apparatus backing them, mutiny on board ships was a fairly common practice if subject to mistreatment by the ship's captain. In smaller social groups retribution is much quicker in human societies.

BALANCE IN SOCIAL ENGINEERING

There is a balance between the actions of the establishment and the liberty of the individual that must be respected by all exercising of authority, which if not respected leads to rebellion. The implementation of the privileged authority granted to those in power must always reside with pragmatic awareness of the inherent nature of the human creature. There is a balance between maintaining social order and both rules and law. Consent and acquiescence must be in sequence to maintain order within society. The understanding of human nature on a deep level is required to maintain the status quo. The isolation or arrogance of the establishment that becomes corrupt, is a critical factor that if breached leads to revolution, the overthrow of authority and often the discredit of those granted authority over others. Hypocrisy once exposed is the greatest danger to all Social engineering. All societies based upon hierarchy utilize Social engineering to a greater or lesser degree. Some Social engineering acquires acquiescence by the populous, such as national policies that create social cohesion to the benefit of the majority, such as a national or group historical narrative that creates a group identity such as the melting pot concept of immigration. However, a much more dangerous type of Social engineering is the division of people by ethnicity or other group identity such as multiculturalism. The old Napoleonic and British Empire social strategy of divide and conquer strategically is a very dangerous position by authorities, since this type of Social engineering thus alienates groups from each other and can become a source of conflict and the downfall of the establishment. Thus, we come to the requirement for social cohesion as the necessity for successful Social engineering.

Though Social engineering has had many differing ideologies; social narratives and terminologies to describe its visionary aspects. Fundamentally Social engineering is the desire to mould society in the image of someone or some group's ideal human existence. Humanities' striving for a new Garden of Eden is eternal. Human Social engineering has very deep mythological and historical roots. One of the earliest versions is of course religious instruction of various types. Classical literature such as writing by the ancient Greek philosopher Plato in his book, "The Republic" and the legend of ancient "Atlantis", or the Middle Eastern religious legend of the Garden of Eden. Sir Thomas Moore and his book called, "Utopia" which came to refer to an idealistic society. There have been many ideal social visions of Utopias and anti-Utopian perspectives which depict a conceptual future or a dystopian world which is a human preoccupation. This is to name but a few of the examples of Social engineering dream worlds. Then there are the political and social engineers such as Karl Marx and various Communists. Social engineering was implemented by the Nazi's via Goebbels ministry of Propaganda. In the former Soviet Union and its satellite states during the cold war. Social engineering goes on today when we have Government ministries that have to do with equality, women, broadcasting or many other non-administrative functions dealing with citizen's persona, private interactions and media narratives. Including minority rights and interference in private citizen's affairs. Other than those laws that provide rules that eliminate contractual disputes and rules of exchange for business transactions. If the Government actively addresses citizen's personal lives and life style, then it is negative Social engineering as I will explain in the ensuing chapters. Chief amongst these ideologies are political and social utopian ideas, the foundation upon which all negative Social engineering rests.

Social engineering in reality can only in the long term be successful if it rests upon a pillar of clear stoic comprehension of the nature of the human being. This is the agenda of proper implementation of Social engineering; to understand human nature. Like a zoo keeper who wishes to be successful, you cannot keep any creature in a barred in cell of captivity to control it long term, without it turning on you; all creatures including humans require a certain amount of freedom. Human beings require certain needs being serviced; equality of opportunity not outcome is necessary. If you want to keep a whale captive you must supply a very large tank filled with water and clearly understand the needs of the creature or it will eventually turn on you and kill its capture, as many public aquariums have discovered. Professional human Social engineering really took off under other names, mainly under cover of Government and business agendas after WWII, but unfortunately for deceptive and even nefarious purposes, up until now it has been a concept that has been used to abuse and mislead people. Human psychology is on the cusp of understanding human nature and needs to be cultivated. Thus, Social engineering by many is seen as the practice of manipulation for the purposes of vested interests. A better use of Social engineering would be to design society in keeping with the needs of people through a clear understanding of the nature of the individual and thus expand those needs to become the way we engineer society's governance for the benefit of society; rather than with nefarious intent or vested interest groups subverting Government as Social engineering is now practiced. Social engineering should concern itself with the necessity to implement a holistic restructuring of society keeping in mind that we have grown weary of the betrayal and manipulation of the social narrative, the interference in our private personal lives for the private gains of others. The sell-out of Government to vested interest and the general betrayal from those that should be our society's arbitrators implementing checks and balances against all forms of tyranny.

We need administration that fundamentally understands our character as a species and not a manipulator that desires to play games with our minds and denies our social needs as a species.

Covert media censorship has become all too common in the western world. Presenting false opinion polls, slanted and manufactured statistics, covering up political insurrection, acts of terrorism and other events have in the past couple decades made the western world appear more like the former Soviet Union; and thus, a shadow of the liberal democracies they once represented. The establishment with their low opinions and condescension towards the working class, are deluded into the belief that their ploys are working. This is a very dangerous social situation given the current economic changes, and the decline in the standard of living being experienced in western nations. The current adaptation of United Nations mass immigration Social engineering policies endorsed by leaders in many western nations in times of economic hardship for the working class, I fear as is apparent at this time are pushing the populous towards fascism and revolt; serious trouble is brewing. "The gig is up, once the methodology has been revealed".

WHAT DOES ETHICAL SOCIAL ENGINEERING ENCOMPASS?

1. The proper implementation of Social engineering is about bridging the gap between policy and human nature, meaning the natural behavior of human beings and designing society to reflect those realities and the determination.

2. The study of what is in the true nature of the human animal is necessary, to be able to implement Social engineering that does not damage human society by being regressive or corrosive to social collaboration.

3. Engineering refers to design and integrity in keeping with human nature. To engineer something is to design something which is functional pragmatically.

4. The study of Social engineering is the study of impact. The impact of decisions, the impact of laws and law enforcement. The impact of law making and the comparative results that emanate from those decisions.

5. The process of law making and the process of creating those laws and initiatives. The necessity for greater forethought and analysis prior to making more or new laws, to consider the consequences more carefully and the requirement for careful analysis. The typical process of making laws is that of an elected legislature putting forth what is called a "Bill". The Bill sometimes goes to a Committee of legislators for review of the laws impact. More often than not partisan perspectives are considered and implemented, though the long-term social impact is not given much thought. This process is flawed in that groups with a vested interest hijack the social narrative in the west and the public agenda by unduly influencing democratic Government in these representative nation states. Undermining public debate and discourse via becoming dominant over impartial review, thus their analysis is fundamentally flawed and prejudiced to a fabricated Marxist or corporate agenda in political perspective that is not pragmatic; as I will proceed to explain this new pragmatism in this book.

6. Law creation and law enforcement often have unintended consequences for society. When a Bill (proposed law) has second reading in some nations in a second legislature commonly called a Senate. To become a law, more commonly, no one ever comprehensively considers how such acts can alter society often with very negative long-term consequences, such as destroying the very foundation of society; that being the family.

7. Social engineering exceeds criminal corruption in the

damage it can cause society in that it has the state take on a religious role in enforcing morality. Thus this type of legal legislation as political change contravenes the principal of, separation of church and state; an ancient principal of Government in western nations.

8. Lack of vibrant and diverse media in nations with state media dominance in many western nations' means that public debate, consideration and analysis is often severely limited and lacking proper impartiality. Dominant state broadcasters often serve as propaganda arms of the state, rather than providing impartial reporting or commentary. Excessive opinion editorializing and not simply reporting the facts has become a common approach. With internet competition changing the nature of media via enhanced competition, these old media as with newspapers are experiencing reduced revenue from advertising sources of income other than the state. Thus, are increasingly beholden to Government to mouth the "party line" of Government. A free press has been replaced by a lecturing press, that only has served to alienate a greater portion of their audience and loses credibility.

Mark R. Blum
2019

Chapter 1

PERSPECTIVE

The implementation of Social engineering requires proper analysis and thought processes. For most of my life I have spent countless hours of study. I have long sought to understand what this thing we call life is, what purpose it serves and how it should be lived. I could see even when I was young that the world is fraught with problems. Initially I thought as is the common perception that the world's problems are a reflection of the social and political system we live under and that the average working-class person is a victim of a society and system foisted upon them. My understanding has changed considerably over the years as I have gained philosophical, theological, historical and personal knowledge backed by pragmatic experience providing insights into human nature and our social realities. I have constantly strived for understanding to interpret the rationale behind life's experience, the human individual, the conditions we live under and our social behaviours.

After decades of careful thought, pragmatic experience, reading countless books, and careful observation I have come to the conclusions contained here. I have studied various utopian ideas from Plato's; "Republic" to Sir. Thomas Moore's; "Utopia", the philosophic ideas of; Karl Marx and Fredrick Engels; "The Communist Manifesto", "Das Capital", Adam Smith's; "The Wealth of Nations" and others. The Constitutions of various modern nations. Anti-Utopian writers such as; Ayan Rand, Huxley's 1984 and many others. Pragmatically I have been involved with various social strata and have come to understand how the world really works in pragmatic terms. Those who gain their philosophical insight in the academic world are often bogged down with theoretical concepts, which have very little relevance to the practical world the rest of us live in. The diminished relevance philosophy once held upon the world, as it has become too abstract. Academics who focus on such issues such as; "The meanings of words", which is only relevant to the language of the philosopher only serve to alienate people from the true essence of philosophy. Classical philosophical issues are far more relevant and in need of revision since knowledge, technology and social change in industrial countries has altered everything and yet philosophy has not kept up. The significance of the ideas of most current philosophers is of little account to the improvement of the world or a pragmatic understanding of it. Philosophy has been hijacked by too many idealists who spent their lives in academia detached from the real world, professors of philosophy and not philosophers. My philosophies are weighed heavily upon classic stoicism and upon the North American school of pragmatism. The world of Ralph Waldo Emerson, Henry David Thoreau, and Henry James, also early European philosophers to mention a few of the great ones such as: John Lock; Immanuel Kant; Hume, Schopenhauer; Friedrich Nietzsche, and many other academics whom have presented philosophical ideas of worthy note which are rooted in pragmatism.

SOCIAL ENGINEERING AND PHILOSOPHY
It is the current lack of the practical application of logic and deductive reasoning (which is philosophies hallmark) regarding important issues such as life's purpose and day to day application in the evaluation of ethical issues which has diminished philosophies relevance and influence upon the world, at a time when it is more needed than ever, due to the increasingly secular society the western world has become. The common pronouncements I hear increasingly that; "there is no right and

wrong," is very disturbing to me. People who voice such opinions have no opinion. Right and wrong is an issue of perspective, of looking at the big picture and the implications of our actions. To be non-religious is not the same as being unethical. I hope to clearly illustrate that ethics are as relevant to the non-religious, as religions assert morality. By determining in logical, systematic sequential fashion answers to the fundamental issues of life, I hope to illustrate that ethics are pragmatic, and that the non-application of them has consequences regardless of one's perspective. While many religions may assert that the non-religious are not moral. I assert that the contrary is applicable, by the foundations I have arrived at with my philosophical conclusions. Many religious practitioners are hypocrites to the theology of their faith, just as many non-religious people are ignorant of sequential pragmatic reality and the consequences of not behaving ethically. Philosophy's contribution should be far greater given societies current starvation and thirst for secular foundations to understand and interpret the world we live in, and its problems.

Though the ideas of British philosopher John Lock and others have had a great influence upon the constitutional development of most western nations and the United States of America. Classical philosophers such as Socrates, Aristotle, Marcus Aurelius and to a lesser extent Plato (who's "Republic" was in fact an oligarchy, and a dictatorship; I find repugnant) have always held a special place in my heart with respect to defining perspectives, in addition to the problems of society and the individual. Renaissance philosophers such as, Rousseau's concept of, "The Noble Savage" and "Rights of Man," also Machiavelli's "The Prince"; establish our struggle to come to terms with ourselves and establish human understanding, social organization, and perspective of our nature as human beings. My primary focus here is the exercise of the realities of the American philosophical school of "pragmatism"; as my orientation. Cartesian philosophical rules are used in my conclusions in that they accurately summarize my perspective for proper utilization of Social engineering. In "Discourse on Method" philosopher Rene Descartes writes:

"Instead of the great number of precepts of which logic is composed, I would have enough with the four following ones, provided that I made a firm and unalterable resolution not to violate them in a single instance."

The First Rule:

> *"Never accept anything as true unless I recognized it to be certainly and evidently such: that is carefully to avoid all precipitation and prejudgment, and to include nothing in all my conclusions unless it presented itself so clearly and distinctly to my mind that there was no reason or occasion to doubt it."*

The Second Rule:

> *"To divide each of the difficulties which I encountered into as many parts as possible, and as might be required for easier solution."*

The Third Rule:

> *"To think in an orderly fashion when concerned with the search for truth, beginning with the things which were simplest and easiest reaching toward more complex knowledge, even treating, as though ordered, materials which were not necessarily so."*

The Last:

> *"Both in process of searching and in reviewing when difficulty, always to make enumerations so complete, and reviews so general, that I would be certain that nothing is omitted. Those long chains of reasoning, so simple and easy, which enable the geometricians to reach the most difficult demonstrations, had made me wonder whether all things knowable to men might not fall into similar logical sequence. If so, we need only refrain from accepting as true that which is not true, and carefully following*

*the order necessary to deduce each one from the others,
and there cannot be any propositions so abstruse that we
cannot prove them, or recondite that we cannot discover
them."*

~ *Rene Descartes* ~

SOCIAL ENGINEERING AND RELIGION

The study of various religions such as; Hinduism, Buddhism,
Islam, Judaism and Christianity amongst other old faiths has
clearly established in my mind that the need for absolute understanding that seems to be endemic to human consciousness. We
have this craving for answers which present day philosophy has
failed to provide in this time of need. The influence of religion
on current western society is greatly diminished as compared
to previous generations. Philosophy now has a great opportunity to fill the void as the questions of the non-religious are the
same as those for people who follow a religious doctrine; yet
philosophy has not yet risen to the occasion, in advocating the
importance of freedom of conscience. Traditional religions in
the past have all borrowed theological answers from philosophy, for centuries. I would venture to state that any philosophical ideas which accept religious faith as a foundation are not
philosophies but rather theologies, though the two terms are
sometimes used interchangeably. Though religious text often
contains timeless wisdom that I see no barrier in citation.

HEGELIAN SYNTHESIS AND PRAGMATISM

Long-term study contemplation and consideration of human
nature have developed; to use a Hegelian term, into this synthesis of mine being a study of Social engineering practice concerning various elements of human existence and the present
framework of society. Binding various philosophic concepts
of human existence into this macro philosophy as presented
which is pragmatic. Stoic pragmatism has been the intent of
all my research and work. Initially my concept was to create
a utopian social organization, which would cure the world of
its ills. Time has taught me that this world really doesn't want

or need a saviour, that utopia is in the eye of the beholder. I have come to realize that Social engineering is often polluted by existing social and ideological concepts, which have been the cause of so much of the world's ills. The concept of the saviour or great leader neglects the key being; personal responsibility. Negligence of responsibility is all too common in current society. The realization which experience has taught me is that the world is the way it is because of the many agendas and interests in society. The world really doesn't want or need a saviour, the world is as it is because; this is the way we want it to be. I attempt to explain Social engineering as concisely as possible. The best I can do is point out the corruption and political-neurosis of the world. I hope that perhaps the realization of these problems will be the first steps towards a healthy world in balance. Balance in my conclusion is the best we can hope for and my presentations are intended to demonstrate why and how this occurs. Decades of experience have supplied me with a realistic perspective of the human condition. Though my intentions have not changed, my perspective has undergone considerable revision to the point that I feel comfortable saying that these are my conclusions and that any additions in the future will be with the same perspective as these conclusions are the result of decades of thought.

Over the years the stoic realization has come to me that the world is as it is because this is the limitation of the current paradigm (synthesis), and only rational realization and reform can change it. The human capacity for self-deception and self-exclusion from liability is an intricate aspect of society's problems. The various interests in society want the world to remain as it is, because they know no different and or enjoy privilege under the current system. The world is intellectually flat in my conception, until we as a society prove that this is not reality; this is the new cyclical and fractal paradigm we must enter. The only thing I or anyone else can do is understand, explain and provide depth to understanding regarding current society.

My explanations, interpretations and stoic observations which will hopefully lend credibility to my theories by being pragmatic; sequentially logical and providing a reflection of my observations and study. I believe this will provide the necessary reform for the future progress of mankind. This has been done in the past by the British philosopher John Lock in influencing the perspective of the U.S. constitution over two centuries ago, advocating respect for the integrity and sanctity of the individual. Einstein's theory of relativity changed our world by opening our eyes to that which is in front of us, often as the expression goes," we cannot see the forest for the trees". I hope to provide a new perspective, this is all that I can do.

CONSCIOUS THOUGHT

I often find that my thoughts seem as seeds in the wind, coming from some collective human thought which collaborates with my minds ideas, which I evolve towards as a result of my experiential education. I often hear pieces of my thoughts expressed by others, where this comes from I can only guess. Emerson in his, "Essay on Self Reliance" said to the effect that, we should initiate our thoughts least we hear them being recanted by someone else. The psychiatrist Carl Jung refers to a collective unconscious. We are all much more interconnected unconsciously than we care to admit. Husbands and wives completing sentences for each other or expressing the thoughts of each other, which were never relayed verbally is an example of that which I speak of; which many of us have experienced. Many of us have had bizarre experiences as I describe in our daily lives, yet we only pause to take so little notice that, contemplation of what occurred goes on for no more than mere seconds. Is this the leakage of the collective un-consciousness which occurs selectively, or is it related to the intensity of the concentration within the mind concerning the matter at hand? I postulate that given time, proof of this will be found through scientific method eventually. Science has already determined that everything is made of energy therefore a subconscious connection is entirely possible, and I believe it will be eventually be found and identified amongst humanity. There must be a common polarity of human thinking for society to exist. Kirlian photography can demonstrate that we all have an aura of energy around our bodies; does this also leak our thoughts?

SOCIAL EVOLUTION

Recent decades have witnessed some amazing changes over such a short time span that they would seem unbelievable to many of us had we not witnessed them. Communism has been proved to be inefficient as outlined in Mikhail Gorbachev's book, "Perestroika" primarily as he explains the lack of democracy and ambition created a state of social indifference and the resulting economic collapse. World wide a frustration with western society within and outside western countries not unlike that which caused the collapse of the former Soviet Union is occurring. Just as communism could not stop the Hegelian Process; neither will the western free enterprise system. This process of social evolution takes place just as evolution alters species genetically.

Public awareness and resulting apathy have become common place as a result of:
- Political lies & deception exposed
- Religious breaches in the doctrine of faith
- Business greed
- A general disrespect for common citizens.

Between:
- The Government and the governed
- Religion and the faithful
- Big business and the customer
- Corporate share holder and corporate manager

This has created a circumstance were the people have come to the realization that; politicians, business and religion serve the interests of themselves and their sponsors, rather than being true fiduciaries and representing:

- The people in the case of Government
- God in the case of religion
- The customer / shareholder in the case of business

MANIPULATIONS

The transfer of power in representative democracies is an ongoing exercise of transferring the power of Government amongst interest groups, as a temporary hostage until the next election. Voting against certain politicians rather than for certain others. The case of religion is rather interesting in that it reflects public apathy as well in that; People have not become less spiritual, they have become less religious (less inclined towards institutional religion).

Corporations herd customers like cattle with electrical phone prods in a system of, press 1 for...press 2 for... etc. Customer service is diminished to the point of treating the customer as a dependant, when in fact the opposite is the case. Corporate Directors provide themselves and their friends with stock options purchased at discounted values and sold by inside trading information. They lie to investors about company income to bolster share prices and dilute the value of the corporation's securities for self-interested financial gain, in a breach of trust against the interest of the shareholders. They undermine investors' valid right to profit. Investors and customers are reduced to a number and the level of ethics is non-existent. An attitude of aristocratic right; similar to the doctrine of, "The Devine Rights of Kings" and arrogance has overtaken public institutions and business corporations. The ethical deficiency of our public institutions has led to public cynicism and apathy not unlike that which led to the dissolution of the former Soviet Union or Arab spring. The renewal of social perspective is an ongoing evolution, and with the death of the past comes a revision for the future.

We are at the dawning of a new type of society and economy based upon technology. It has become apparent to me that at this point in time we seem to prefer to treat the symptoms, rather than the root source of our problems. The assumption that events occur in isolation is prevalent. A comparative analogy would be that of a person becoming ill with cancer as a result of environmental chemical pollution in their home, receiving therapy to eliminate the illness, then returning the person to the contaminated environment where their body acquired the toxic illness. The crimes of corporate sponsors of the state are ignored, while Government focuses upon the weak and poor with Social engineering. Symptomatic cures are a false science that ignores the root cause.

In dealing with criminality, usually the response is that society should become tougher in its dealings with social problems often based upon incomplete perception and assertions barren of facts. Draconian remedies are often implemented wholesale upon even the innocent with new laws. This leads to spiralling social injustice and tyranny upon the majority. Going back to my previous cancer analogy; this is comparable to saying, "let's increase the dosage (drugs) to cure this person", then the patient dies from the cure! Incorrect symptomatic treatment is prevalent in all facets of our society. Common sense and Psychological doctrine states that in order to solve a problem the person must first admit and recognize that a problem exists and its root cause. The solution can only be found by looking for the foundations of our social ills, analysing them and arriving at conclusions based upon these findings, this is what Social engineering should attempt to do. The necessity for philosophy into the new millennium is; to re-establish ethical values by demonstrating the realities and benefits of those values; reflecting real life experience.

HYPOCRISY

Life's present-day realities are determined by our strengths and weaknesses. The repercussions of different options and courses of action, in honest critical concise assessment need to be pursued. Look at the options in terms of new direction. Discarding that which has been proven to not work, in a pragmatic sense and present these conclusions with logical pragmatic solutions. This all sounds very lofty and yet most of us already do this on day-to-day bases in our personal lives. But what if your options are limited? People can and have been dominated by military and various types of brute force throughout history. When society operates by hypocrisy and injustice the end product is rebellion which destroys it by rotting it from within. The cold war did not destroy the Soviet political system; neither did military conflict. Social decay caused by intolerance for diversity and indifference by citizens no longer engaged due to hypocrisy destroyed it. Tyranny always decays society to the point that it collapses in on itself. No need for a "cold war" just leave it alone to die a natural death from its self-inflicted wounds.

INDIVIDUAL SOVEREIGNTY

Society must recognize the sovereignty of the individual. Will we, and can we ever create a utopia for all on this little blue planet, or are we too uncivilized and un-sophisticated a species? Our society is rampant with social critics, however criticism or pointing out folly without recommendations for reform and change is irresponsible and usually interest driven. To point an accusatory finger is safe because attention is deflected from the critic to others. The illusion of neutrality adds power and influence to the critic's commentaries. However, my experience is that critics usually induce their behaviour for gain, either personal wealth or interest oriented.

Fundamental change is necessary; How we can improve our political and social institutions to be more democratic, pragmatic, productive and inclusive to eliminate rot from within, which like termites can leave the surface looking solid but the structure is ready to collapse? The perspective within this book is of a general nature, and not cast in stone in order to present flexibility as a result of circumstance. It does not matter how idealistic we are; economics and human nature are issues that must be dealt with as pragmatic reality, to do otherwise is to invite long term failure; communism is an example of just such a failure.

The demise of communism is not proof of the superiority of any other economic system; it was a self-inflicted destruction. A lack of innovation, opportunity, and motivation by citizens will destroy any society by rotting its foundations. Progress is essential for continued existence just as the human body starts disintegrating when the growth of youth stops. This fate also affects free enterprise societies economically as will be demonstrated. Free enterprise is derived from a natural state for the human being, as trade is the foundation civilization was built upon. Intellectuals such as Adam Smith have explained the operations of the industrial economy, but free enterprise has always existed as a normal behaviour to which people naturally gravitate. The world is now the shopping market of the technically informed. Money, hardware, and even knowledge can now be transferred around the world in seconds, with or without free trade the world has changed. History teaches that technological change is economic change and causes social restructuring. My intention is to outline a strategic and cognitive process to comprehend fundamental issues and comprehensive philosophic perspective. My process consists of:

1. Starting with pragmatic experience and understanding basic human nature.

2. Following sequential patterns to devise symbiotic political, social and economic policies that are performance and outcome based.

3. Using logical deductive reasoning to review human ethics; morals; false lineal thinking and reactions to potential policies.

4. Advocating the processes of a modified version of applied project management to pre-evaluate all Social

engineering prior to implementation and analysis of human psychological studies to comprehend reality and human nature as fundamental to social engineering.

5. Equating rational perspectives relative and relevant to human existence, and document social models of history. Like consideration of the Roman bread and circuses policy of social appeasement and other examples of human history.

The variety of reforms and policies which must be dealt with can only be addressed via sequential thought, which will constitute and comprehend the entirety of our social construct. Certain conclusions are deducted for how they affect other aspects of the social construct.

Society is part of the comprehensive structure of all existence, nothing occurs in isolation and all actions have a domino effect upon society, which is seldom obvious. That which claims to be reform which does not use pragmatic sequential logic and careful analysis of effects can and has often been extremely detrimental to society, thus is not an improvement. Opinion based policy has had a very negative impact due to the political social construct that has evolved by this Social engineering. Social engineering which does not follow this formula is based upon un-vetted opinion most often and is metaphorically equivalent to claiming mathematical expertise by a person who doesn't know the formula to add numbers. The formula for accurate Social engineering as in mathematical addition is that:

1. Each inclusion of fact of human nature adds to a perspective and does change the formula results.

2. The result of all Social engineering does affect society with additional factors. Using this social formula this we must exercise caution for without taking care negative social , economic and political decline can result. It is my belief that greater public involvement is another

57

solution for this issue.

3. An elite ruling over society always leads to this group becoming social   ly isolated and thus creating social problems based upon ignorance of the prevailing social conditions.

BACKGROUND

Within these writings I anticipate the reader will gain insights into the most relevant issues of Social   engineering in a very personal way regarding the rationales of life. Some people will undoubtedly be upset about my perspectives and conclusions; however, my experience is that any annoyance will be the product of vested interest which foresees its own extinction, has no desire to change, because the status-quo always creates and serves vested interest with advantage. I am not attempting to create a religion; only a perspective and system of analysis which validates itself; faith is not relevant to Social   engineering. By presenting these standards for social   change, I hope to lend credibility to scientific pre-analysis, by establishing standards for the pursuit of authentic, pragmatic and positive social   change. What I have attempted to do is create perspective and understanding of life as it presents itself everyday under the current paradigm, and possibly change our perspective by giving Social   Engineers the template for the requirement to perform more cautious analysis in the making of laws or policy; and create an awakening as society and the political elite in particular at present are apparently not conscious of the detrimental effects laws can have upon society in general.

Social Engineers need to also contemplate the role of both public and private incentivisation upon society. Financial incentives are commonly utilized by Government's presently; in the form of reduced taxation and or inversely, as financial awards granted to the population by Governments. There are a whole host of justifications for their provision, however in essence as in the old Roman policy of "Bread and circuses." The motivation in western society is with the intent of Government seeking public favour for an incentive awarded to the voting public. I do distinguish this type of policy as being different from the implementation of new social policies such as for example the implementation of a national health care, or a free education regime. Which is social restructuring via being an electoral platform, and thus a social /political determination. Distinguishing the two from each other is often convoluted by politicians. Since this is a form of wide scale social and political bribery of a nation's population. This can be an ethical slippery slope, as it often is in that: If Government creates law and policy based upon financial incentives for the population that are purely wealth distribution initiatives. Then the ethical dilemma for politicians is; why should the political elite not also seek financial incentives for themselves overtly or covertly personally, or on behalf of their political party, from vested interest groups? The most common response I would anticipate is that; "politicians accepting such money are accepting bribes; this is contrary to their fiduciary responsibility to the electorate." Yet both of these practices are common today in almost all western nations. If one is unethical, isn't the other? Both policies in fact I believe are unethical; since the political determinations of the people should be determined by the desire for social change; motivated by social acquiescence; as a democratic social determination invoked politically. Regarding the politician we would say' "This is unethical and unacceptable contrary to the politician's obligation to act exclusively as a social fiduciary." This analysis points to a type of highly insidious social and political policy that often gets Governments elected currently; that is at its very core insidious; yet is commonly determined as acceptable by the population at large in self-righteous indignation. We are as this illustrates, often our own worst enemies. Such policies are only ethical if initiated by a plebiscite of the payers with an opt out provision; meaning these are matters that the electorate should decide and have an option to not participate and choose an alternative, otherwise this represents extortion foisted upon those who do not wish to participate. Government programs almost never offer choice. Those who in fact may have other preferences must without options participate with the herd in a one size fits all strategy. Yet, for some bizarre reason that which government does with your gross salary tax contributions, even if it is something you are supposed to benefit from; you never have any say or option regarding your participation; governments make determinations and it is in most instances the citizen never has the provision of even options that fit their particular situations uniqueness.

A negative birth rate is clearly an indication that something more is sociologically, very wrong in western society. Something we as a society need to think about and question as I have. If my presentations are social ly pragmatic, logical, functional and sequential, then they are undeniable; for faith is the realm of religion. Pragmatic functional sequential logic is my method in the search for the truth. Scientific approaches use reproducible verifiable experimentation to validate hypothesis. This is a formula I believe that is complete and self-explanatory, with basic deductive reasoning, There is no lack of evidence in terms of multiple scientific studies that validates the reality that most Social engineering has been manipulative by vested interest, by minority groups utilizing political correctness to obtain social advantage for themselves, that has no regard for the effects their actions have had upon society.

There is currently a lot of referring to environmental degradation, due to perceived world over population. Hypocritical political globalism seeks to allow greater third world immigration to supplement the first worlds loss of domestic population due to low birth rates. If a reduced population is an environmental advantage, then populations should be permitted to decline in the first world with no immigration inflow. I have a primary concern with mass third world migration as it is the removal of talented, educated and motivated individuals from societies that have a short supply, and a real lack the skills these individuals have; which are needed to reform and improve the standard of living in third world countries. The west does not need more third world doctors, who become first world taxi drivers; because their credentials are not recognized. How can we expect the third world to advance and improve themselves when their political reformers, dissidents, and educated professionals keep migrating to western nations? The third world's brain drain is an authentic travesty of our times, that further impoverishes these nations by extracting valuable human resources. This is a new form of western colonialism in many regards; causing untold suffering in the third world.

These decisions are politically made by politicians like bank bailouts of corrupt financial practitioners back in 2007 where in governments knowing the cause was massive lending fraud, and excessive leveraging of mortgage backed securities, by the banks themselves; the politicians resorted to cronyism over fiduciary responsibility to the nation's people. Rather than bailing out the poor with tax payer's money, by nationalizing the borrower's mortgages in the 2007 financial crises; thus, preventing a lot of families from ending up on the streets and homeless. The political establishment resorted to massive bank bail outs, and what is clearly an amnesty for crimes committed. In the usual manner it is the working classes that ended up with; and are still paying the bill. While banks once again earn billions of dollars in profits. This circumstance, I think once and for all established clearly in the minds of citizens in western nations who their governments truly represent.

The decision to bring a child into this world is a positive affirmation and optimistic decision; it is a confirmation of the health of society and faith in humanity. Biological reproduction is the natural aspiration for all creatures from the smallest microbe to the entire diversity of species upon the planet earth. When human society chooses not to bring forth children, the implication of such a decision are a clear demonstration of biological decline based upon nihilism and a species that lives in pessimism; it is both an inditement and conviction demonstrative of social   decline and illness. While food production and technology have decade after decade increased worldwide to meet human needs, food shortages have only occurred in nations with extensive political corruption and malfeasance. Authentic optimism sees humanity as overcoming its challenges with advancing technology and social   lies to overcome the current challenges. Clearly as always' "actions speak louder than words". Thus, current western society has been overcome by a spirit of pessimism that may prove given the present course of events to be a self-fulfilling prophesy, under the current circumstance. Given the current trajectory of western technology and innovation, space travel and settlement will most likely require more innovation and a larger population to achieve this ambition that may involve terraforming other planets in our solar system. The current circumstance is destabilizing western nations socially and politically. Failing to recognize that technological innovation can only occur in a stable society and that all this political destabilization being created by policies of the ruling class and their "group think" is very dangerous. Though I must admit that the current social   war being created by the ruling class I predict in all likelihood will backfire upon them and cause the population to consider the elimination of representative "democracies" with Swiss style direct democracies; which will be much to the establishments chagrin.

Karl Popper's book, The Open Society and Its Enemies provides an analysis of these questions of democracy, and I believe we are seeing the death of all kinds of "philosopher kings" from Plato to Marxist utopian ideologies. Before there is reconstruction, of course there is usually a period of mess that proceeds project completion. Thus, I must admit I am optimistic that these issues will sort themselves out positively; otherwise current political circumstances will lead to another collection of ruined human constructions, and to another dark ages of deprivation and misery in human history. Archaeological digs demonstrate that the historical path of human civilization has repeatedly disintegrated due to corruption and leads to the repeated demolition of human social and political constructs of the beautiful creations of the human imagination. The question is one of; have we learnt how to rid our societies of tyrants and totalitarian corruption by despots? I believe that it is time for human consciousness to come to the realization that only by taking direct responsibility for Government and Social engineering, can we achieve the creation of an environment where the nature of the human spirit can flourish. Your utopia is someone else's hell! For every attempt at utopia, be it communism or some other ideology; utopian ideologies have more often lead to mass murder and social destruction, for there is always the question of what does your utopia do with those who disagree with your new order of society? This one issue has resulted in the end of the twentieth century creating the greatest period of mass murder we know of in human history; thus far. Government demi gods have repeatedly demonstrated the need to control people via social engineering being utilized to manipulate the people; as the tendency of Government is to control our lives, even against our wills; and to become corrupt on behalf of vested interest. Unfortunately given its potential for good, Social engineering has also more often than not also been abused on behalf of psychopathic vested interest. The proverbial canary in the social "coal mine" has gone silent and died, it's time to exit the current mine paradigm and; - *reinvent ourselves in the west.*

Chapter 2

INSIGHTS

Much of what has been presented thus far has been an historical review of where our society has been and is currently. The objective format of this has been to progressively build my case for the following advocacy regarding ethical social engineering. The prior chapter and introduction were historically oriented. Commencing with Chapter three the pace will change to focus upon where we need to go to make social engineering an ethical practice and the perspectives necessary to achieve this change. I will starting in Chapter three to begin building the case for the reforms and social epiphanies necessary to have a program of ethical social engineering. This chapter number two summarises where we are now. The following Chapters from 3 onwards concern; - where we need to go.

SUMMARIZING MY PERSPECTIVE THUS FAR

Social engineering in the form of "political correctness" is cultural Marxism and multi-culturalism; a form of divisive identity politics through covert manipulation. This is presently being employed to manipulate society into divisive groups by a vested interest who are seeking economic, social and political advantage for themselves, and the undermining of the concept of meritocracy. Those who espouse these ideas frequently attempt to silence dissent by utilizing pejorative insults towards those who see fault with their ideology (insult is the first sign of weak argument). Social Marxism espouses false social narratives, creates divisive villanization of individuals and is revisionist of both social and historical narratives. Unlike an egalitarian melting pot social model for immigration, these ideologies also promote divisive multi-culturalism that is a perspective to promote the isolation and ghettoization of ethnic groups. Much of this is utilized to justify discriminatory affirmative action policies in employment. A society that appoints privileged individuals to political office, loses touch with the majority of their citizens, and is detrimental to social cohesion. The results of this thirty-year social experiment in the west are in. Given the current electoral results in most western nations where the dominant political parties as a result of their policies are being voted out of office and loosing support to an angry population, it is clear there is at present a disconnect with the ruling class that has occurred. Proper Social engineering practice seeks clear perspectives to bring social concerns in the light of day, rather than its current status as being exercised covertly, and foisting division upon society as though we live in some form of regressive dark ages. Affirmative action can only occur where there is no discrimination already; thus, it is unnecessary.

It is important to point out what it's not, as much as what Social engineering is. Failed economic, social and family policy does clearly demonstrate that greater study and care in implementation of laws and policy are necessary to ensure the integrity of all facets of the current political theatre. When a society's birth rate and family life of citizens is undermined to the point of facing extinction, this is a clear sign that there are serious social problems in the political system and that Government is failing to serve its citizens adequately in some capacity. A nihilistic society is a society with serious social problems, as this is clearly contrary to all Darwinian precepts of species continuation and survival. This is a problem with contemporary western society as there are government activities that clearly must be controlled. There is widespread cynicism that has also taken place with the political system in the west in general. Disbelief in the integrity of the political system is now widespread in western society.

Previously social engineering sought to mould society, which may, or may not have any bases in the real world, but society does suffer from cause and effect, when it is implemented. Social engineering has been conducted by both the nation state and religion, historically having collaborated in a very unholy alliance. Religion requires faith and presents itself as absolute truth. In most western nations Christianity suffers from a credibility problem that occurred prior to the loss of credibility by politicians and the political process. Politicians have attempted to fill this void with legislation and that has only led to the current political crises caused by their failed attempts at Social engineering via legislating morals and ethics. Clearly there is a need for political reform. In fact, it is my belief that the process of reform is well under way as alternatives are explored in the next few years and coming decades. This is currently having an enormous impact on the history of the western world with respect to social organization. Since the beginning of human existence, fundamental questions of organization have been asked, and philosophical perspectives have been used to answer them. Civilizations, nations and other social organizations, including religions have been created out of various philosophies. The influence philosophical perspectives have had historically has created the greatest human civilizations, from ancient Greece, to the United States of America. Religions have used philosophy to justify and interpret their doctrine; from Christianity using philosophy, to the Chinese quotes of Confucius. The fifty years after WWII known as the cold war; was a battle threatening world annihilation over the philosophy of totalitarianism Marxist/Leninism Vs free enterprise and elected representative nations. Most human conflict is caused by self-interest of social groups based upon a particular philosophy. War reflects our lack of cohesion in human thought; someone is always trying to impose their will and ideas on someone else; because they feel arrogantly superior, overtly or covertly. Scientific paradigms update previous theories which are really philosophies until scientific method is applied. A hypothesis is really philosophy; not science. Scientific explanation provides validated truths and not theory as is hypothesis.

1. The paradigm is where in new ideas; such as Einstein's theories of relativity, revised Newton's scientific (hypothetical conclusions in terms of the previously accepted laws of physics.) Scientific paradigms can shift due to better information coming to light over time, nothing is stagnant. Conceptual fundamentals are based upon the informational resources of a time. Another common element which still links science and philosophy is the issue of perspective interpretation.

2. The application of a pragmatic logic and using a sequential scientific method and perspective concerning any aspect of society, is a rational concise interpretation from the perspective gained, as a result of the available information at the time, having the ability to alter the human perspective based upon changing circumstance and control. Predetermining Social engineering's effects by careful study prior to implementation is essential; so that Social engineering does not become a tyrannical science.

PRINCIPALS OF SOCIAL ENGINEERING

Perception is truth in the eye of the beholder. Perceived truth is relevant, even if it is delusional. It is a belief based upon experience either from imagination or physical sensation held by only one person or a group of people. The colour-blind person sees yellow as green. This is the colour-blind perspective, it is no less valid than the perspective of the majority. However, society exists on normal perspectives, in order to be able to function least it dissolve into anarchy.

1. "Normal sentiment" is the functional perspective society operates under. To not operate within this perspective is to be viewed as invalid (possibly labelled insane). It is the rationalized functional perspective of a particular society and the material cognitive world. The majority must function under normal conditions. Normal is the avoidance of extremes between lack and excess, the mathematical average between polar opposites of behaviour.

2. Ideas held by one person, or a minority of people differing from the majority are initially in conflict with conventional thought. Paradoxical deliberation which is not pragmatic or logical can be invalidated sequentially via analysis of historical facts.

3. The history of pragmatic logic and sequential analysis has proven majority opinion to often be false. I.e.: Proving the world is not flat; proving the earth is not the centre of the universe. These are some well-known paradigms of history.

When the ruling establishment's perspective becomes a differentiated view from the majority belief in society, this transforms society, by creating dissent that in the long term brings down Governments and transforms society. A study of revolution would quickly determine that out of touch leaders create more rebellion than any other source. Usually it is as a result of out of touch policy initiatives, for which the population has had enough of. Wealth can create a social bubble where in the ideas of such individuals can become dominant only within an isolated social class; that seem like taunting the people. When leaders lose touch with the people's pragmatic reality.

Through clinical analysis, the scientist and philosopher advances societies' understanding. Perceptive philosophers see society as it is pragmatically functioning and can see the paradoxes which are altering human perspectives; to become new paradigms. Philosophy is differentiated from science, in that it interprets the implications of discovery with hypotheses that must be tested to become accepted as an approach to problems; to explain phenomena and ideas. While the scientist discovers physical truths, the philosopher uncovers perceptive realities that go on unnoticed. Philosophy goes beyond science in dealing with the abstract and supplies the interpretation of the consequences to the physical world; which may or may not be proven by scientific method; which relies upon the ability to see, feel, and touch; that which others do not notice until a philosopher brings attention to it. Philosophy experiences paradigms just as science does and has its own formula to acquire truth utilizing sequential, pragmatic, logic. Philosophy deals with perception and possibilities; *not necessarily validated final or absolute conclusions.* The possible paradigms and epiphanies of philosophy are never and can never be known, as they are limited by the rules of philosophy and social evolution, history recounts, that it is results orientated. New philosophic perspectives are like the view which changes the higher up a mountain you climb and the location of the mountain Vs being on the mountain. The peak has never and may never be reached as each paradigm is merely a different perspective governed by human evolutionary pragmatic reality. If you want to deal in absolutes, then acquire a religion; that is what religion is about. Science is technical, and most practitioners do not like to review ethical, social decisions, their implications and interpretations of change, or suppositions. Technology is changing our awareness as is research into human natural variation and behaviour. The current ethical debates about when life manifests itself, and the human social issues of the present time, in an increasingly secular world, demonstrate that philosophy is needed more today than ever before. In previous generations religion gave absolute answers, which most people accepted, so critical thought was not exercised; only compliance to fear based upon superstition. New scientific developments create ethical implications in genetics, social organization as a result of science and technology for example. That we must be willing to re-considered in light of the implications. The future of mankind from here on will depend upon society to determine how to transform the future and what form that future will reconstitute into.

People in the west have long believed that western society had freedom of speech. The advent of the internet and censorship via closing the accounts of many very popular YouTube channels and Twitter accounts in recent years has demonstrated that trying to change the traditional news media's narrative is not tolerated by many. YouTube creators find these social media platforms have demonstrated a willingness to shut them down when requested by Government. Advertiser and Government pressure has been exercised with impunity in recent years to close many politically controversial creator sites that have been shut down by the platforms themselves; working collaboratively with the Government. While the main stream media loses audience, social media's independent voice is growing. The Government's actions to request social media web sites shut down certain individuals' perspectives clearly demonstrates dissent is not welcome. Initially this new technology caught the establishment off guard. Given the revelations of Edward Snowden, a former computer technician who is exiled in Russia to prevent his imprisonment for his "whistle blowing" that exposed mass population surveillance and monitoring by The United States Government, utilizing social media's information. Exposing that the Government monitors everyone's social media and personal email activities via computer spy programs. It is clear that mass monitoring of all internet activity including everyone's computer meta data is currently practiced covertly. This type of wide scale monitoring also occurred in East Germany with their secret police the Stasi. In fact, the Stasi it was revealed after the collapse of the East German state proceeding the fall of the Berlin Wall; that their Social engineering included efforts to sabotage people's personal lives and prevent those they saw as opposed to the state by undermining and interloping into their personal lives. Ensuring by their interloping that these individual citizens would not succeed, in any job applications, and even school attendance. The Stasi apparently covertly sabotaged citizen's ability to improve their lives, in covert retaliation due to opinions that the communist political establishment did not desire vocalized. This type of censorship causes social stagnation and eventual collapse. At one time in communist East Germany it is estimated that as much as 1/3 of all citizens spied on their neighbours, friends' families, including children being taught at school to spy upon their own parents on behalf of the Government. Now that we know that western Governments are monitoring their citizens activities; it leaves one wondering. How long until they use this information like the Stasi; as they are currently doing this right now; in a more moderate fashion.

Free discourse is transformative and self-correcting for society. Without free speech society becomes stagnant, errors in political and social policy fester and politics can become intolerable creating volatility in society. A volatile society can lead to draconian counter cultures being created that lead to often tyrannical politics. Free speech is the pressure relief valve of physical violence. It is the testing ground of the appeal of what may or may not be consensus perspectives for society. It is also the most peaceful war humans employ. Violence is the human response to the lack of proper and available discourse. Thus, repression of free speech is an invitation to violence and rebellion eventually.

Chapter 3

HUMAN NATURE, TRADE & EXPLOITATION

There are no people who are better engaged in the pragmatic world than those of us who are or have been entrepreneurs. If the entrepreneur does not see events with brutal reality and street smarts s/he is not long a survivor in business. The history of the world and civilization starts with the investment into the business preoccupation of trade. Trade takes many forms and manifestations.

Social engineering's intention is to manipulate society. It is important that Social Engineers have a clear stoic and accurate perspective of what they are managing; that being social systems based in law that have a foundation with; human nature. There are many types of Social Engineers, be they politicians; religious figures or business. Most current day Social Engineers want to be covert and hide the social control social control foundations and the long-term implications of their activities. Social engineering is not necessarily nefarious; in that it can be very beneficial to society. In casting light upon these initiatives and properly performing pre-analysis of these activities which have potential to alter society. This writing is about the foundations for a more scientific approach to Social engineering that are stoically in keeping with human nature. If there is one characteristic of human nature which is overlooked, it is the significance and importance of trade in human interactions. No study of Social engineering could be complete or accurate regarding human nature, without some commentary in reference to the high level of significance of trade. While academics who have spent a lifetime in the cloister of universities may overlook this aspect of human life, few who live outside such a sheltered existence would consider this to be an irrelevant topic. Policies, legislation and belief systems have in the past, and do in the present tense, alter society in very significant ways. Sometimes these seats of the pants initiatives can be very detrimental to a society; thus, they must be implemented with great care.

Even prior to the sixteenth and seventeenth century in Europe, explorers from Marco Polo to sea fairing explores; all who interacted with others knew and understood that even when encountering a different culture; with a different language; in a different environment; that these peoples would entertain one thing which is fundamental to all humans; and that is trade! They always brought as basic provisions trade goods that could be exchanged; as a door opener to a new relationship. It is too often overlooked, but all humans engage in trade. This is a foundational principal of Social   engineering, business; and all advanced civilizations on this planet. Trade is more than business; it is the understanding of human nature. From a foundation of trade, we built relationships; we built societies; and finally, cultural practices and laws that set the rules for that trade activity.

When Samuel de Champlain arrived in the new world in the early sixteenth century an informal trading relationship already existed between French and other free traders from Europe and the natives, for almost a century. When Champlain arrived to establish a colony the first thing, he did was trade with the natives for furs they harvested, in order to help pay the cost of his voyage. Champlain also left young European boys behind and took some native boys to Europe who would live within each other's countries pending his return to America. Champlain gave the European boys the mission to learn the native language, so that when he returned the following year, both he and the natives would find it easier to barter for furs and trade goods. These translators would help cement a trading relationship that would endure hundreds of years afterwards.

No one taught either the natives or the Europeans that trade was good; they understood this universal truth from pragmatic life experience. Just as entrepreneurs to this day understand that trade is a good way to improve your life. This is an indisputable human truism concerning the nature of human beings; it is as simple as that.

Since the beginning of human existence what we refer to as society (the structure of cooperative organization by people) has coordinated itself into what is commonly referred to as "civilization". The real definition is that of a system of organization for trade purposes that creates ground rules we call business regulation, social hierarchy and culture. This describes the prevailing method(s) of physical enforcement and psychological manipulation through indoctrination to comply with the doctrine of this structure to follow a pattern created by being pragmatic. The very foundation of all civilizations and societies are defined by rules and regulations of trade and thus social interaction. Under society's structure, these rules vary little throughout the world from one social environment (culture) to the next, but the foundation in trade always underlies human relationships. Trading relations with certain tribes evolved into Champlain becoming involved in native battles (at Lake Champlain), against the Iroquois Confederacy as trade leads to friendships and alliances.

The particular values a society accepts as relative truth are determined via society's particular historic, technological, economic and or social bias towards trade. Hierarchy is based upon brute power, psychological manipulation, maintenance of the status-quo to control trade, customs or as is usually the case; a combination of these factors is a defence against modification, to protect the status quo (those people with wealth and position on the intergenerational administrative top of the social spectrum). Society is structured to provide the self-serving maintenance and survival of a system against those who would alter it by not complying with its rules and customs. Government gets involved to justify taking a piece of the activity of trade for its own purposes and social organization of trade works hand in hand. All societies proclaim themselves to be the epitome of the ideal state; to do otherwise is to acknowledge the need for social reform, this occurs in most countries. By proclaiming moral, ethical social superiority and attributing the status of all citizens as being the result of that structure. The state solidifies authority by co-opting collaboration with status.

Our society is based upon trade and exchange, yet most people are hindered in this process, by being foisted into a Socially Engineered program of debt enslavement, which starts with student loans and or mortgage debt; that by design entraps them into a life of servitude and a new form of serfdom by design. This matter of mortgage and other debt slavery is how the establishment works. The establishment's indenture through debt utilization harvests trade's profits, by diminishing profits via overt and covert confiscation. Through charging mortgage interest imposed to implement central bank monetary circulation because money is created presently with no foundation, other than the borrower's pledge to pay interest and principal on that which did not exist without the borrower's pledge as security for the loan. Money is created on the backs of workers labours, thus creates wealth which is economic expansion. Taxation of wages and trade; finances the state along with resource extraction royalties. All money is the result of productivity from trade, extracted from the workers. Creations and human resource efforts cause the result of activities we call trade to be initiated by society. Bank creation of money is the printing of new currency, when adding exchangeable assets of value to the economy, funded by Government adding to the currency in circulation in the form of primarily mortgage loans. Assets are things and services we perceived as being desirable to acquire, so as to become a commodity of exchange with retained value; by barter or provision of currency. We trade in order to possess things and services. Thus, new assets grow the economy and new currency is needed, that reflects commodities available; which is an expanding economy; as a result, currency is created; as is productivity. Charging interest upon production; as banks do, creates inflation, because it lacks intrinsic value and thus interest charged upon homes and major purchases is an inflationary tax upon economic growth. Because interest does not increase the value of the home, but rather is only a cost added to a home purchase; interest charged has an inflationary effect upon the economy. This also hinders capital accumulation, and availability that if not paid in interest; would be available for the average citizen to create a stronger economy with this additional capital interest removes from the economy. Interest removes capital available for additional investments, or purchases by consumers in the economy. But due to this parasitism in banking, the working class are impoverished, and enslaved. Capital accumulation is not possible, because the interest charged spans decades of lost opportunity for economic growth. Adds decades of servitude to these loans, that is a non-refundable rental fee, which parasitically keeps the working-class poor all their lives. There is as this demonstrates a financially lucrative vested interest, and reason, to not teach finance in public schools.

USE OF FORCE

In a reciprocity-based defence pact between the people and the establishment to secure the profit from trade away from theft, the state believes it is justified in demanding taxation and the utilization of the lives of the nation's naive youth to maintain the status-quos position, usually via military action. The youth, if they survive military deployment, often end up being bitter when they grow older and wiser, realizing that they are not a part of the social fabric, but rather were used by the hierarchy, defending their monopoly to control trade and reap profits. Though this is seldom discussed beyond academic circles, the reality is often that it is societies disenfranchised and disadvantaged who predominate in the dangerous activity of military enlistment and action. They often return from the vile activity of human conflict; upon decommission are often betrayed and forgotten by their country. Abandoned like a worn-out machine thrown into the scrap heap of social poverty, families are left shattered, minds damaged, bodies with disabilities. All this inflicted upon the naïve youth for the establishments military adventure. Like the American Confederate troops defending the plantation and slave system during the American Civil War; few of these recruits owned slaves or plantations. Beyond the defence of one's home territory from invasion, military adventure would not be entertained by any intelligent self-respecting adult of greater years. The responsibility for the results of military damage fall upon the society which put some of its citizenry into such a position. The price is long term (often lifelong) financial support for those injured in conflicts and the families which are destroyed. The long-term obligation for the costs of war are ethically far higher than those compensated in most nations. Being drawn from societies disadvantaged classes they become like so much of our world; discarded like some piece of refuse. While military action sometimes becomes necessary pragmatically, society has a high long-term financial obligation to its victims and the cost upon a society which acts ethically towards its obligations are much more than the cost of the original conflict in the long term. However, like with so many acts of human behaviour, negligence rather than acceptance of the obligations owed is more often the case. The maintenance or creation of a social structure is the real agenda of military action, rather than the higher values of humanity usually cited, for this reason mankind's violent nature may never be diminished for all human societies are based upon vested interest, sleight of hand, and the threat of violence towards those who threaten the position of the status quo. Justice in international conflict is as elusive as justice within the domestic jurisdiction of nations. Fundamentally the indoctrinated soldier is often more of a victim than those they may kill in the performance of their duties. The soldier sells his personal ethics and peace of mind and becomes a tool in the interest of others (the status quo) who seldom have any genuine appreciation for their intergenerational personal sacrifice beyond hollow ceremony.

Has intergenerational war improved the quality of Europeans, by acting as genetic selection eliminating those members of society with the most violent tendencies, making current generations less violent? Has it diminished naivety as a genetic trait improving the quality of subsequent generations? Perhaps this has something to do with the current consciousness of Western Europeans. If Darwinian Theory is correct, then violent tendencies would eventually eliminate themselves by the rules of natural selection diminishing warriors over time as a result of so many millions being killed from generation to generation in their early youth and never having children. I seriously doubt this; however, the thought is a possibility. Human resources, like capital and material resources are utilized in exchange for nations to justify taking a piece of the trade profits of the economy by the state. All wars have at their root a trade-based justification. A subsidy to justify the middle man; known as the state. Politics is sleight of hand to divert attention. War is eternal for a slow development of the human pre-frontal lobe enables old people to exploit youth for their wars. Much of that which government presents as acts of benevolence are not benevolence, but rather shrewd acts of self-preservation to maintain social stability in their own vested interest. This charging of interest creates lethargy in the economy, and has a tremendously negative economic impact, as it does not liberalize the availability of capital resources for new business creation and expansion. Consumer purchases spawn greater economic growth and financial circulation of currency through encouraging greater economic diversity, in addition to reducing the negative impact of inflation by being based upon authentic trade. Interest charges are unproductive; and very inflationary by devaluing currency through dilution.

LAW VS. JUSTICE

The very foundations, of what is known as; "The law" is not the administration of "Justice" *(the system misleads and deceives society by stating that justice is its purpose; this is a deception).* The reality of law is that it is a system of preserving the status quo as are most Government institutions by misleading human resources to believe that the system cares about their woes. Perception is the individual's reality, but perception is almost always in error for it does not account for another person's perspective. We all have different perspectives; we can only agree on those matters of common experience or comprehend common experience, even experience changes with perception of the experience. Humanities arrogance of perceived knowledge is the veneer covering reality.

In the study of Social   engineering, Justice is a very important factor as it is fundamental to one's social   perception of society; without authentic justice, society is not civilized but rather barbaric. Justice lays down the pragmatic terms of the social   contract between the state and people's perception of the legitimacy of the state. I define justice not in terms of the politically correct movement's perception of equality of social outcome, but rather in reality as the fair and equitable financial access and application of the law; in enforcement, pronouncements, and conclusions in a society, which provides equality of opportunity. Outcomes are the responsibility of the individual to create under a system of equal treatment and opportunity. It is not possible to have a system of "Justice" when it's provision is neither equitable nor fair in its foundations (though to my amazement many naive people believe a day in court is the acquisition of justice). Conclusions of present-day courts are based upon penalties for breaches of the law. All law has a commercial foundation, the sleight of hand is an assumption that society is fair and equitable in its' social organization when it is not; this invalidates many convictions for legal breaches as being with regards to the concept of justice. Law in its present form is a set of rules without ethical consideration forming a foundation, which only serves as a systematic program of maintaining the status quo, as it's only bases. True justice cannot be served up like a meal by courts or laws; - it must be founded in pragmatic reality.

There is a significant difference between law and justice. A society with justice can only be a way of life coordinated with equal opportunity, (this does not refer to affirmative action; which is reverse discrimination ignoring qualification). Equal opportunity for access to the law is non-existent because it depends upon financial ability and deep pockets, authentic justice must be merit based, and not held hostage to the financial cost of legal counsel, or justice does not exist; otherwise the terms of reference are fraudulent as a foundation. This is not a pronouncement that society should exist without rules and regulations. It is however an indictment against the current system which has a foundation that ignores the root causes of antisocial behaviour in favour of zealous enforcement of a society with superficial glass walls. Improper Socially Engineered utilization via vested interest driven agendas, social blockages against individual self-improvement, upward mobility and a deficient provision for mental dementia or very low IQ's, which in many cases is the cause of a great deal of that which we refer to as crime and imprisoned individuals. The judicial system is slanted to ensure that those with wealth from trade always have an advantage by ability to afford good representation; it is a manifestation of wealth. Currently western society's judicial system in it's out dated design is composed of 15th century customs, in desperate need of Social engineering to correct it. The western judicial system is one without authentic justice, as it ignores pragmatic reality with respect to the necessity for an open path towards upward mobility for the talented or ambitious individual, and fair treatment for those born with social disadvantaged. Social engineering mandates the realization of political reality as an intricate part of justice, and to separate the two is a system of injustice – mere law and thus very primitive, even barbaric! The current system in most of the western world is fundamentally society being irresponsible for its own crimes against human nature, by side-tracking the reality of its own incompetence and negligence when it elevates legal issues and ignores social reality under the assumption that the system is righteous, and society is fair; which it is not! There is a lot of malevolence in this world, which is the obligation of any justice system to control.

The industrial revolution was initiated in England first historically, this has been attributed to being because of greater commercial and personal freedoms, but not in their rival country of France. Excessive Government bureaucracy delayed France's industrial development until much later. Industrial development was very socially disruptive and led to the civic battles even involving the English military exceeding the troops utilized in the battle of waterloo to put down street fights and riots with the Luddites, who found their home-based crafts-based business enterprises being undermined by mass production. Industrialization led to tremendous social change, including in Ireland and Scotland for peasants, and tenant farmers who were often forcibly removed from their land (tenants to historical English immigrant landlords); by excuse of a potato blight, and thus millions died from starvation, were killed, or moved to America; as a result. Much of this event was engineered by the establishment, so that land owners could replace people with sheep; to supply woollen mills. There is always a cover story like in this case with the potato blight; to deceive society via false propaganda. While famine was occurring, Ireland was exporting other food stuffs; potatoes were not the only food produced.

The entire system is bought and sold by those with wealth who can afford to pay exorbitant legal fees. The poor and working class are financially blockaded from any form of justice. But the matter is much bigger than simply the exorbitant financial cost which prevents many from its acquisition. The system itself is completely flawed as it can be summed up as; may the best debater (lawyer) and the deepest financial pockets win. The system makes pretence of being fact based, but the facade is the ignorance of the documented evidence; all too often and too distracted by a focus upon the facade of drama created by lawyers. Case Briefs that contain evidence should be the focus of a system which is fact based, not drama and gamesmanship; as the current system is a fiasco. Perception is the individual's reality. But perception is often in error; for it does not account for another person's perspective. We all have different perspectives, we can only agree on those matters of common experience or comprehend common experience, even experience changes with perception of the experience; as does the passage of time, and reflection combined with revelation of facts change; to reflect reality in the shadows of life.

Until society incorporates human nature based Social engineering, and pragmatic reality that is unvarnished and fact based as part of its judicial foundations it shall continue to be unjust! I am not saying that all laws are incorrect necessarily, or past Court Trials are all incorrect. I am saying that the root causes are often the essence of legal breaches that get ignored. The process of legal determination should be performed in an office environment of case briefs being examined by judges as most of the aspects of a trial are only impressive to illiterates and those who like drama over substance. Public broadcasting would also ensure everything is above board. The reality of society, of judicial tyranny; too often occurs in the shadows!

With proper Social engineering nipping problems in the bud, society can prevent many future problems; life behaves as a domino effect. An unjust society for example may lead to a life of crime as in for example, a childhood of poverty or mental illness. The issue is not one of breaches of the law, or the elimination of poverty, as some social activists may claim; though those who gravitate to a philosophy of social ism might present such a perspective, with a certain degree of accuracy. The issue can be as simple as giving away something to someone who is lacking for less than the cost of an overpriced prison system that serves no long-term value at present; locking people in cells is no solution, only punishment and a temporary prevention of mobility system. In keeping with the preceding frame of thought concerning the big picture of the system as an entity. The system is only concerned about your morale as a participant within the system. Providing the illusion of participation and inclusion; otherwise you might rebel. These are the issues western society has great trepidation in exploring. None of this was designed by accident it is all intentional.

JUDICIAL TRIBUNALS

The Social engineering of the judicial system: The inadequacy of the current western legal process is in some regards recognized in many western nations. This is clearly acknowledged by the trend of Government to create quasi-legal entities called Tribunals. I do not endorse these entities, though I have personally attended many as a landlord. My experience is that they certainly achieve the effect of simplifying law enforcement and reducing costs. My chief complaint is that they do not have any professional law trained representatives often determining the cases brought forward. In Canada we also have human rights tribunals, that I have been advised also suffer from the same lack of professionalism. We need to realize that these semi courts do have powers to award financial rewards, they are not really a Court of Law. The main issue I find here is in what these Government entities admit; that the legal system has evolved because it has failed to be authentic; and needs serious Social engineering to correct it.

THE INDENTURED SOCIETY

Slavery can take place either by shackles, economic indenture; or credit as is more common at this point in history. The very foundation of all societies and human interaction is based upon pure unmitigated self-interest founded upon trade. From the most primitive to the most technologically advanced, all societies are built upon a system of trade and exchange, this comes from the human need for reciprocation; without reciprocation, disenchantment will always occur. The "buy now pay later" scheme; by payment of interest that compounds to two or three times the principal as occurs with mortgages is a plan of indenture as it adds decades of unearned value that exploits the borrower via what historically can only be seen as usury. This kind of indenture was the feudal surf scheme. The modern version is the charging interest on home mortgages for money obtained mainly in collaboration with Government; the independent bank is a lie and myth.

At the turn of the century, North American Governments wanted to settle their interior, and in so doing increase agricultural production of the nation as a whole. The Government enticed people mainly from Europe who were the best qualified for agriculture in a northern climate. In Europe land was in limited supply thus offering free land to the heads of households was a very attractive offer to get something that was not available in Europe. The Government even went so far as to provide tools and provisions of food which is much less known, to help these people get a start. Some of the land was covered with trees and sometimes stones and they had to be cleared by a great deal of hard manual work by the settlers. Let us not forget the land was taken away from native North American peoples, after conflict, and or disease introduced from Europe. French Canadian history has suggested a correlation with children arriving in the colony spreading European childhood disease. Europeans had a primitive non-existent comprehension of the causes and spreading of disease and no concept of what created immunity, at that time. Given several years the settlers-built houses, barns, cleared fields and planted crops. Few Europeans objected to this type of social policy, because it was founded upon the principal of reciprocation. The result was the building of the America nation, and the return to the nation was many times the investment. "Indian wars" was a phenomenon in the United States of America. The fur trade's cooperative history between the American Natives and French-Canadian fur traders created a different relationship that resulted in the facilitation of peace and land treaties in Canada that avoided the kind of conflict created by the agricultural land grab that was more common in the United States; resulting in a different relationship with Native Americans in the lower 48 United States. Also, several centuries of intermarriage with French Canadians, made a more common cause by familial connections with Native Americans. This was the Legacy of Champlain's record of creating good trade relationships based upon mutual respect.

Trade and exchange are a reality of human nature. It has been my observation, that most conflicts arise when someone feels they are getting a raw deal, and then conflict arises. Entire volumes of human history, revolution and warfare can be traced to have an essence in the anger of a people who believe they have been, to use the popular term "screwed" in trade and a retaliation in court is started to restore what is perceived as a theft. However, acts that have Government collaboration such as mortgage indenture, are not seen as usury, though all creatures have a natural right to a secure home. This causes massive poverty from the indenture being created, and the excessive cost of home ownership by causing inflation that reflects the true cost due to interest being added to the cost of purchase, caused by interest-based money creation and circulation, creating price inflation as this money filters into the economy. The profits of

Mr. Mark R. Blum

banks (interest) hurts the consumer by destabilizing the value of assets with interest driven inflation. The homeowner always loses out because the true cost of a home is the combination of not just the principal paid upon the loan, but also the tremendous interest paid by the borrower. Consumers are often ignorant of this reality of costs that this is a scam. Home buyers fail to realize that over the amortization of the mortgage that most often two to three hundred percent in interest will be added to the principal payments over 25 or 30 years. The consumer always losses in the selling of their home, because they ignore how much interest they paid. Home purchasing with bank financing costs thousands to rent the purchase financing,

UNDERSTANDING SOCIAL ENGINEERING

I started my Social engineering research at a very young age with the idea of Utopia, that mythological concept that all mankind's' ills are created by social structure. After years of pragmatic social and business experience, I have come to believe that all Utopias are doomed from inception. The human mind is capable of deceiving itself into believing that if only we had different architecture; different social organization such as socialism or communism, shared the same beliefs or religious faith. If we made provision for equality and made everyone the same, if only people were not so selfish or self-interested - that we would be living in a wonderful world of peace and tranquillity. My discovery through years of reflection, study, observation and experience is that all these ideas do not work pragmatically. The entire thought process from which they derive is from a state of delusion. From Plato's Republic to Karl Marx and all those philosophers in between and after, the objects of their ideological philosophical infatuations are the unattainable. I dismiss large portions of their ideas as, heresy to reality. Only the human mind can deceive itself into such a maze of deception based upon fantasy. No other creature I know of is capable of creating such pillars on quicksand (due to the incapacity of animals to think abstractly like a human). Our abstract

86

thinking is often contrary to our pragmatic reality. The premise with which these and many other philosophers start is incorrect. The questions, which they ask, are invalid. The question is not one of what would be or could be the perfect society. The correct question going forward is what is the natural state for the human to live in? How can human nature be facilitated to enable the human being to fulfil the potential of the species, as nature has so provided an inclination and ability? The human being is unlike other creatures with respect to:

1. The ability to communicate in complex and abstract terms.
2. The ability for fantasy.
3. The ability for delusion and self-deception, self-interest, the egocentric factor.
4. The faculties and physical ability to imitate and create complexity.
5. The ability to go beyond the natural limits of our physiology.
6. The ability to dominate the planet.
7. The ability to facilitate cooperation of the species beyond the pack   (compared to pack animals) into entire armies.
8. The reliance upon social   interaction and cooperation for mental stability and maintenance of the species physical needs.
9. An intergenerational perspective.
10. The ability to create a socially altered paradigm, which is evolutionary in nature.

SUMMARY THUS FAR

Though our homes are often built by others or exchanged, I do see a very exploitive act emanating from feudalism to this day, and that is charging interest on home mortgages by banks and third-party interlopers, also Government subsidizing this. Central banking should be reformed to have Government fund interest free mortgages and end the financial feudalism that resembles share cropping. Removing excess mortgage indenture with government interest free mortgage loans would free up capital for private citizens to encourage their participation in the free market and thus increase trade productivity encouraging individual agency and independence.

The current interest charged upon mortgages is a system of social engineered covert serfdom. Any person with a twenty- or thirty-year mortgage amortization schedule would quickly see how money games in mortgage lending is far more profitable than productive acts like home construction; that's why it exists. Home ownership is to me a natural right we need to accommodate, and I can see huge benefit for the economy to leave economic feudalism behind once and for all! It is important to recognize that very little occurs by accident and that all these systems are created by intentional design. The average person starts their work life with this tremendous debt to acquire necessities such as a mortgage for a home that has decades of interest added to it; student loans for an education; car loans for transportation etc. The necessities in a western nation commence being acquired prior to family obligations. Clearly the poor start life far behind, the wealthy who often have the benefit of being given such advantages. This indenturing of citizens is an unproductive activity that removes productivity and impoverishes people. Nations currently inexplicably grant money creation authority to central bankers, who create money for which interest is created out of thin air without any commodity of exchange being created that balances the two. Interest; money circulated must approximate commodities that are exchanged, or it exploits the payer via un-earned value. Therefore, interest causes economic inflation, as it circulates money that has no foundation in productivity of retained value. Money is not a commodity as in a durable good. Money is a different species, it is a medium of exchange. Not a durable creation; though some might claim it is via a deceptive shell game of calling it "capital". Interest is an expense, not a manifestation of capital, even if reinvested it still causes inflation in the economy. Because the money goes into circulation, that created nothing but more money; money with no substance always creates inflation as money supply thus exceeds goods available.

Government charges the borrower for loan insurance and adds this to the principal in most cases. The central bank advances newly created money to borrowers who all pay interest. The only one paying out of pocket is the consumer. It is a shell game that enriches all the parties except the consumer who pays back over decades of indenture in what amounts to two to three hundred percent of the original loan as interest. While the consumer is the only party to secure the loan, it's a Social engineering scam that is a continuance of feudalism or share cropping, both being exploitative on a massive scale. No wonder the mechanism of money creation is not taught to the general public in school, who are in effect being exploited. Rent or own a home, the fact is the costs of this system are born by every citizen. Therefore, the poor remain poor for the most part.

Business deducts interest as an expense, thus reducing income. Consumers pay interest on their homes, and in an act of cognitive dissonance pretend it is not a major cost of home ownership; which is in fact paying a rental fee for money from a bank who borrowed the money with the consumers equity and pledge to pay and thus receive the mortgage funds from the government's (or privately owned) central bank. The true cost of home purchasing is far more than the purchase price, that being the loan principal. The resale price does not reflect the true cost of home purchase finance in terms of how many decades the loan payments will be in the form of mainly interest primarily. Look at any twenty-five to thirty-year mortgage amortization chart and you will clearly see there is decades of labor that is paid to the bank; This interest paid to banks for money that was the government's, impoverishes the working people. The

Mr. Mark R. Blum

system is rigged for extra ordinary profit and usury in the form of artificial interest. Governments could lend mortgages in fact at no cost to their people interest free. Forcing banks to pursue their authentic purpose of capitalizing business instead. There are no accidents here, this is clearly engineered indenture; the average person is blind to this reality!

Chapter 4

MANKIND'S NATURAL INCLINATIONS

P roper Social engineering has an obligation and critical responsibility to fund and conduct research to uncover mankind's fundamental natural state of being in an ethical manner, uncovering the pragmatic effects Government and social alterations invoke prior to implementing any program of incentive or disincentive programs and laws. The determinations of the domino effect of our actions are critical in order to create long term success, and not cause serious harm to society and the individual. The key to this is respect for diversity of personalities and orientations which nature has created. If we are to believe in Charles Darwin's Origin of the Species, then we must accept that variation in our species as individuals is then normal, and if we are to be pragmatic, then we must be careful that rigidity in social and political policy is not inappropriate in approach when designing laws and any social policy. Essentially tolerance for diversity is in keeping with human reality. The belief in natural selection is not a determination of diminished validity of faith, what is called superstition or religious belief.

Natural selection is a presentation that we are all diverse as individuals and I have yet to meet a human being who does not authentically subscribe to his or her uniqueness; we each know instinctively from pragmatic experience that all human beings are of a variety and separate states of consciousness. This is not to say that there is not a strong possibility that there may be other forces at work also, such as a collective un-consciousness, which I personally believe there is tremendous possibility that human society and collaboration has some element of beyond societal norms, that extends to some form of electrical mental linkage that occurs between people. Some call this; "gut feelings", I theorize it goes deeper than this.

Imagine you are a zoo keeper say for example; you are responsible for the care, maintenance, breeding and wellbeing of polar bears. Do you create a desert environment to house your bears, or how about a tropical rain forest to house your bears? How about a marine environment? These comments of course are absurd, and any thinking person will automatically dismiss them outright as ridiculous; and correctly so. In the context of human social development and social structure, this is exactly what we have been doing. We have tried everything from the tropics to a marine environment. This is what I mean when I referred to the human condition of delusion. Continuing with this line of thought; as the zookeeper you would first need to educate yourself; on the environment from which any creature under your care are native of, and their natural state of being; your mission as a responsible and caring zookeeper would be to duplicate as closely as possible the natural environment of not only bears; but also the particular type of bears under your care. So, with this metaphor in mind; what is the natural environment and nature of the human animal? This question becomes very difficult to answer with regards to a human being because we are more complex than any other animal due to the following factors:

1. There is the crucial problem of different cultures, mythological beliefs, technological change, self-deception (arrogance), intelligence, self-interest driven agendas in conflict, fantasy against the natural laws and the social nature of the species.

2. There is the human capacity to mould one's environ-

ment - invention and creation.

3. Human beings are flexible and diverse, this severely complicates this matter, but not beyond our capacity to utilize broad strokes. What this means is that we must avoid rigidity in our implementations.

If we choose to observe the "natural human" such as may be found in a hunter gathering society, we are further misleading if we think that this is human nature as they all differ in custom and way of life. Though there is always a fundamental similarity in terms of behavioural characteristics. Humans live in all manner of environments from tropical to arctic conditions, therefore are very adaptable.

DEFINING ELEVEN HUMAN NEEDS AND NATURE

One thing we can count on is diversity of social and physical structure, sometimes due to the political or natural environment, and sometimes due to systems of belief. The key of course is one common element, and that can only be the ability and need for the human creature to have, a sense of biological and mental progress. Even regressive religions and philosophies have this element of progress within the confines of their belief systems in that they present their regression and control as progression and improvement of the human condition. Human history has shown certain consistent behaviours, which are the repetitions of history; such as the following fundamental needs:

1. Respect for diversity of our personalities, characteristics, our life style and our nature as individuals.

2. Freedom to conduct trade with others.

3. Freedom to pursue ambitions and material needs for one's self and family i.e.: food, shelter and clothing. We have a natural right to security of our homes as shelter from authoritarian or legislated seizure or theft as a natural right, like all creatures on earth. Though this has long been violated to create indenture and create lives of

insecurity imposed upon people.

4. Security from theft, fraud and deceptive practices; malicious or murderous behaviour.

5. Respect for diversity by protection from the imposition of behaviours in public display which are antisocial in terms of respect for other cultures.

6. A sense of advancement and improvement, as satisfied by the need for personal growth, be it physical comforts, or mental development of our minds.

7. A right to self-determine our biological procreation and relationships

8. Mental improvement through the free acquisition of knowledge, information and exchange of ideas.

9. Freedom of movement; Freedom of choice, and freedom from restraint in these pursuits.

10. Life without a legal confinement or undue restriction upon our ability to fulfil one's desires affecting one's self and personal life, that are not involuntarily affecting others of sufficient maturity to make such determinations.

11. Freedom from repression of our liberty, to self-govern our economic initiatives, progress and the prioritization of meritocracy over privilege.

DEFINING SEVEN HUMAN NATURAL ECONOMIC ACTIVITIES

Put a limitation on these requirements and rebellion will ensue given time. This is the Achilles' heel of all utopias in that they are a formal structure, which inhibits human nature and the previously mentioned basic natural needs as criteria. The fundamental questions which must be determined are issues surrounding; what is the genetic instinct of the human animal? Just as a cat, will dig a hole to bury its dirt. A dog establishes a hierarchy in the pack, and other creatures follow an instinctive, genetic code of behaviour. We do not need extensive studies to understand our basic nature, thus the foundations of our governance. The following is a listing of basic human economic activities:

1. TRADE: All human beings do one indisputable thing constantly and that is sell, trade, and exchange.

2. MATING: A man makes a presentation of his qualities to a woman in exchange for union, and a woman determines if this is what she wants - and vice-versa. Regardless of claims of love, it is in reality; infatuation with qualities available for exchange. Fidelity and trust are also qualities to be desired. This is of greater value than wealth and position for long term success; loyalty and bonding come from shared adversity and long-term fidelity.

3. THEFT: A thief takes things covertly through sleight of hand by using trickery or deception and without payment, utilizing force or deception for personal or business gain without integrity. Also included is extortion, as in the case of subversive theft by Government taxation without consensual authorization. This is a common human activity.

4. CREATIVITY: a person makes a product or provides a service and supplies it to others in exchange for money or barter as in the case of business or an employee.

5. INVESTMENT: The act of taking a risk utilizing capital to build something by intentional design with the desire and intention to reap future rewards that increases the original investment to an amount greater than savings will generate.

6. EDUCATION: Acquire knowledge and supplies services. A person acquires specialized knowledge or performs another person's perceived drudgery for exchange.

7. COLLUSION: The corruption of political or business activities to acquire a vested interest from politicians via financial incentive covertly supplied in exchange for protection from legislation or acquisition of an opportunity to pursue a financial benefit outside of the public interest for self-benefit. This is also an aspect that business and corporations also engage in.

NEGATIVE HUMAN SOCIAL ECONOMIC ACTIVITIES:

HUMAN WARFARE

War is often the product of theft which is aggression in all societies for extortion there are; Physical wars, legal wars, political wars, social wars, and economic wars. The more mature the society, the more developed the practices of exchange, the greater reduction of the need or desire for war like behaviour. War is defined as force being used via brutality or threat of brutality to extort something from another person or group that is not supplied by free will. All forms of war are detrimental to society and civilization; though evolutionarily educational.

THEFT

Theft is an economic activity along with collusion because this does occur in reality as an economic activity and is very lucrative, thus a scourge upon human society as it is abusive of trust and lacks integrity. When nothing is expected in return, the recipient gains enormous profit (100% for nothing). The offer is so appealing that many subscribe to corruption and society must have such protections in place legally as to penalize such acts severely given the tremendous temptation.

IDEALISM WITHOUT FOUNDATION

On all levels of exchange (trade) takes place. Everything including a person's body and character is something, which is bartered for favour; we are all involved in trade. Communism and social ism is unrealistic in that it ignores human nature for a group based ideology that sees social strata as the machinery that creates wealth and ignores human nature; without fair trade we all become thieves. These ideas have not, and cannot work in the long term, and only serve to steal from the productive with little to no return. Anything received without some form or expectation of remuneration for services or provisions rendered is exploitation of the inventor, creator and the productive, unless supplied voluntarily as a cooperative agreement.

A BRIEF HISTORY OF TRADE

Be it peaceful or malicious, the inability to be and do all things aptly sums up the human need and natural tendency for exchange and trade. To not recognize this self-evident truth a person must be truly living on another planet amongst a different species of being than the human being; away from all human reality. We live in a world of Social engineering were insincerity, fraud and fantasy has replaced pragmatic reality. We need to reassess many of our social issues and see how to make application of these concepts pragmatically. This is human nature the social animal; we are not evil, we are not malicious any more than a wild beast kills another animal for food out of hunger. What we seek is fair and equitable relations. Trade is a fundamental aspect of human nature. Giving something in exchange for something in return is as old as humanity itself.

I can make good spears and you have potatoes; how many potatoes would you give me for one of my spears? I will return with more spears if you are fair in trading with me. If I get cheated, I will avoid you, thus you will be poorer as a result. Steal from me and there will be war that has a potential to hurt or kill you; therefore, is very risky. When the Europeans set out at the age of exploration and knew that they would meet with unknown peoples. What did they determine they could do to establish relations? They brought trade goods and weapons for protection. Without a common culture or language, they knew trade would be understood, weapons would aid in or provide protection from theft. It was not brotherly love that brought them together -It was trade! The natural state of the human species is that of living in a circumstance were trade and exchange is a fundamental and everyday affair. Thus, even the most undeveloped societies always have a public market for trade to take place.

Some early human societies and individuals were historically very warlike and conduct trade by theft and brute force, some by peaceful counter offer as history has demonstrated. War carried a great risk, for human beings' object to theft, thus the thief in early human history put the thief's life in jeopardy, as those who were stolen from might just kill you, and even your family for sabotaging their family economy, so this activity is very risky. Peaceful trade is always far superior as it keeps manufacturers alive to keep producing the items of your desires. Regardless of the techniques, trade is endemic to human social interaction on all levels, be it peaceful or malicious. The inability to be or do all things aptly points to the human need for exchange, which every human by natural necessity recognizes. When theft becomes rampant; production stops; which creates poverty.

A RELIGIOUS TRADE CONTRACT OF ANCIENT HISTORY

Most of the ills of the world can accurately be summed up as problems which deal with trade. The Judeo/Christian Ten Commandments are an example of the contract for good business relations with the mythological God:

1. You shall have no other gods before me.
2. You shall not make for yourself an idol.
3. You shall not misuse the name of god in vain.

This is a firm notice that God's contract is exclusive, that loyalty and trust are required and protection of gods good business name in item 2 & 3.

4. Remember the Sabbath day.
5. Honour your Mother & Father.

These items above are an exchanged reward for your part and a bone to the establishment of families which is fundamental to society.

6. You shall not murder.
7. You shall not commit adultery.
8. You shall not steal.
9. You shall not commit false testimony.
10. You shall not covet your neighbour's house.

These are fundamentals for a superior Social engineering framework for peaceful coexistence trade, establishing regulations for a well-engineered economic environment and relations establishing honest fair trade.

CLASS STRUCTURE

The utopian ideology of communism and social ism has built the entire context of this perspective upon a false premise; class struggle (or today's "Patriarchy", class terminology). Class being in the context of the European Aristocracy and business elites I would not deny that class structures definitely exist. I question their authentic economic validity as they are the product of perceived superiority founded upon inheritance. Productivity overcomes class; as many feudal estates went bankrupt after the industrial revolution in Europe. Men of trade and commerce began to "own" the aristocrats vote in Parliament and the House of Lords as is the current practice. The landed gentry lost peasants labours to the competition of industrial production; feudalism thus collapsed as an economic model. The mortgage indenture of industrial workers is its replacement for exploiting labour.

Talent, ability and items for exchange have often overcome class restrictions and facilitated entry into other classes in exchange for talent or because of wealth accumulated. A notable exception is the Indian subcontinents caste system, which holds back the untouchables from self-improvement based upon caste over merit, talent, intelligence and ability. Though current legislation in India seeks to reform the practice of permanent multi-generational concepts of inferiority.

REVOLUTION

Revolution has historically been a particularly effective method for belligerent monarchies or classed societies. The French revolution's use of the guillotine is a good example of the way in which belligerent class-based societies deal with this injustice eventually. Revolution may be rare, however when it occurs the repercussions are severe for establishments which restrict upward mobility. At any time, there can only be a limited number of individuals with accumulated wealth, however to hold back innovation via taxation and thus trade, is harmful to all society by causing it to stagnate. In addition to holding back innovators, it also turns them in to the enemies of the establishment. Few things are as dangerous as an intelligent innovative enemy, it is always wiser to assimilate them into the establishment and allow society to naturally evolve. This is the fundamental strength of present-day representative states, in that they hold the belief that the people are in charge theoretically, and that only ability and talent based upon trade determines the different social strata. We see this took place in Europe where the industrial revolution took hold under British constitutional policies of free markets versus the experience during the same timeline in France being held by the aristocracy and bureaucracy. Equal societies with differences in industrialization initially due to different types of Government.

MARXISM

Discrimination based upon intelligence and talents is acceptable by all people throughout the world; if it is validly applied; after all who would want a deficient doctor operating on them; or a airline pilot who is inept etc? Class based societies are highly repressive in keeping the lid upon upward mobility through a small crack in the fabric. Communism also recognized talent in the arts, academics and athletics in an oxymoron against their claims of creating an egalitarian workers society in addition to having privileged elites of party members. The society which Karl Marx wrote about was at the beginning of the industrial revolution, peasants manned industry under horrid and brutal administration. The effects were strikes, rebellion from mistreatment, and labour negotiation, were yet to be recognized in this type of trade. I believe that if Marx could see the modern industrial state, he would rescind most of his writings as historically incorrect assumptions based upon a particular perspective of time. Though China's current industrialization under communism is a flash back to the tyranny of early industrialization in Europe from the times of Karl Marx. In an example of irony, I am refraining here from getting too deep into the delusions of Karl Marx's ideas.

INNOVATORS

A fraction of all people are innovators; the Avant-garde. I consider them to be human variants as this behaviour is not the norm. These are the people who create the business jobs, make social advances, and are responsible for the inventions, arts and are captains of industry. Yet what do we do to these people? Current society discourages and undermines them, to the average person they are a threat: Offended and threatened in the face of ambition and or genius, the human being is at war with himself for the sake of his own ego to the detriment of his own well-being. Innovation is the seed of trade, business; and thus, jobs and new opportunity innovation, thus feeds society forward as it builds upon itself.

THE THIRD WORLD; POOR NATIONS

Third world countries export via migration their innovators and ambitious to first world countries and so remain impoverished. Like a vacuum sucking up all the talents and the potential for improvement of the third world to venture forth. Talent swells industrial countries as refugees and economic immigrants from the third world. They are the politically outspoken and technical innovators, once in the west they seldom return to their homelands after all, why reinvent the wheel when you can use someone else's; it's much easier. The responsibility for the third world brain drain is heavily within the hands of people in the first world who think they are doing these people a favour, when in fact this is false virtue signalling, robbing these nations of a critical and limited human resource for development. These people are the rebels and dissenters who could organize opposition to a corrupt state. As a result, the cycle of third world poverty, and mismanagement continues as most of the innovators are in the west, where third world doctors become janitors or some other position below their abilities, because the west already has plenty of them; who are even better educated. Meanwhile in their home countries people die in the millions as a result of a shortage of physicians and a loss of a lot of their ability to bootstrap their society.

Class determining financial wealth is still believed by many. Status created by inheritance has been the greatest hindrance to social   progress ever accepted by mankind; where competence is usurped, mediocrity rules. Social class and inheritance (vested interest) is viewed as superior to talent and intelligence by arrogant plutocrats. Progress and improvement is hindered by a lack of capital for small business innovators worldwide. Our technology has exceeded our social   perspective; media repression manipulation via technology of political, economic and social structure goes on. *Nothing has changed; only our toys!*

Chapter 5

SOCIAL ENGINEERING
THEORY & PRACTICALITIES

Social Engineering via education in a regimented structure is the reason. The German Prussian Government began offering free Government operated education; as it aids the states militarism. Line up and follow the teacher's commands; raise your hand before you speak, the Government determines the curriculum, and you must eat that which the nation sate has determined is its prerogative you learn and stay in tune with these requirements of the education system; all traits necessary for a good soldier; obedience! Education is used to indoctrinate future workers, create regimented citizens who are indoctrinated to follow routine and regiment, to be followers not create innovators or facilitate talents. Academic subjects are taught which will never be used by the majority of the students in a grand waste of time, money and resources. Pragmatic education in real life, the operation of the economic system, and the promotion of talent is ignored. Natural talents are ignored and never catered to; uniformity and control is the intent of present-day education of children, indoctrination is practiced. Knowledge of the media and current affairs are barely touched; if ever approached at all in the school system. Those subjects which are taught are provided in a slanted fashion with biases the state wishes to place in the minds of children. Free thinking is squished to promote assimilation and conformity. We have mediocrity because this is what the modern state churns out, in their industrial mandarin factories called schools; in Universities they now indoctrinate students teaching neo-communist "repressor vs Repressed" ideology. The system has betrayed tax payers and the perception of the youth of their ancestors. The family is being villainized with a narrative of presenting men as repressive. Your children are being indoctrinated to often disrespect their parents while the parents pay to financially support their nemesis. By the time your children graduate from school, you have funded institutions that regimented them and indoctrinated them, to disrespect you and their minds are filled with what is often distorted information. Half-truths and lies of history that is edited for other purposes. Here are some basic oversights of current education:

- Did you learn how to budget your money?
- Did you learn about machinery and basic automobile maintenance?
- Did you get an unbiased education about history, such as labour rights and the struggles to end economic exploitation?
- Did you learn about the legal and political system and how to defend yourself in a court?
- Did you get an unbiased education in personal health?
- Did you learn about statistics for raising children successfully such as the poverty created by single parent households?
- Did you learn about banking and both business and the stock market?
- Were you taught self-reliance?
- Were you given an education based upon your interests or talents?

These are personal issues of which we all should be aware of. The list of pragmatic skills not supplied by schools is very lengthy as demonstrated. Schools ignore innovation and talents in their students in favour of creating communistic uniformity, thereby as in the defunct Soviet Union they tried to diminish individuality and enforce the social Marxist narrative of society controlling the social narrative to indoctrinate perspectives for their Social engineering. The same intentions follow religious education systems that indoctrinate children to a certain perspective, as in the middle east and third world nations.

SEARCHING FOR TALENT

Society should instead be in constant search for talent and intelligence like Tibetan Buddhists search for the reincarnated Deli Lama. The state controls thinking and descent with a structured study program, cherry picked to only present their politically correct perspectives; rather than free study. We have mediocrity because this is what the education factory, like all factories churn out; the exact same product from every individual. They are useful for the Industrialists and financiers of the political machine who control the levers of representative elections. They don't want taxpayers to know how the political system is owned not by them, but rather has been sold to the corporate industrial financial elite who fund the political parties. The politicians must repay their debts somehow to the establishment. The only thing the political process delivers is mediocrity for the maintenance of the status quo, which is why regimentation is the way schools are intentionally designed. Educational Social   engineering has been going on in the western nations for a very long time, by intention it serves various purposes of the state. I am casting a conscious light upon what has been really going on.

The advocating for patriotism has unfortunately always had a militaristic intention. I do not oppose nationalism, because it espouses local control over government; rather than trans nationalism which can only lead to totalitarian dictatorship. The more authority vested in local government, the more democratic it is likely to be, in that direct democracy creates greater social cohesion, better governance would most likely follow.

Mr. Mark R. Blum

THE POLITICALLY CORRECT WORLD OF TODAY

A society of media parrots is the end product of the current western education system; rather than free thinkers. The mass of people awaits the radio or television news broadcast to give them an opinion; otherwise they would not have one. They do not have the education for critical thinking because the system held back the perspective a real education would supply. A truly educated population in pragmatic reality might become troublesome on the factory floor. Corrupt government policies in the early nineteen twenties was followed by the Great Depression. Realities like this and many other historical truths are not permitted in school because this still occurs. If knowledge is power, repression of knowledge is more powerful. While many facts like this are known by the educated elite who have studied extensively, the majority of people are ignorant, because the only education they have is state supplied directed and controlled indoctrination. The IQ test is used to measure potential for academic achievement. This is done to streamline (pigeon hole) a child who will be placed in either unskilled (semi-skilled) or skilled designations of study. Talents are ignored and never facilitated, ability to think for one self is not accounted for; truth and pragmatic knowledge is ignored, innovation is not accounted for; creativity is not accounted for. Like a cattle roundup, the industrial state moulds and controls its citizens minds in countless deceptions and pre-set limitations. The industrial state has simple minded ethics and morals limited to; the maintenance of the establishment and financial profit. Innovation is encouraged in limited fashion as a necessary evil because it intimidates the establishment. However, without continued innovation western society would collapse into an economic depression and they know this; it is a two-sided sword.

HISTORICAL SOCIAL ENGINEERING

History is all there is; we don't know the future; we do not know the present; everything is a comparative of the past. The visionary must sight the past as examples and metaphors of the future least his ideas are inexplicable. We all live in not the present and not the future but rather the past; this is reality. The building blocks of our future are our perspective and knowledge of the past. The present will only be invested in if past success and or failures are known. We deceive ourselves into believing that we are living in the present. We can only modify the past as it is our dictionary for all existence. The past is ever changing, and we seldom interpret it accurately for values and perspectives change with time. We cannot be fair and understand the past by using the values and perceptions of today only the perspectives of the time provide an accurate picture. In order to interpret the present & history we must know the history of history.

A good example is pre-world war two Europe and North America, both societies of racial and religious bias and intolerance. World war one was ended with the implementation of the "Versailles Treaty" by a generation wishing to reverse historical disputes and animosities with neighbours and destroying the German economy for years thereafter. By being unjust towards Germany with severe reparations for a war they did not create, but which arose from a European system of alliances which dragged the entire continent into conflict. The provisions of the Treaty of Versailles combined with the destabilizing effect of the great depression and sowed the seeds of animosity in Germany to grow a Hitler (an opportunistic Austrian veteran of WW1) and initiate WWII, or shall we say Chapter two of the same war. The true cause of the war is only written about in scholarly works of history to this day. Hitler repeatedly riled up the German people by sighting the "Treaty of Versailles"; the loss of territory; the confiscation of territory and resources; the payment of reparations which bankrupted the country creating the greatest inflation in world history in Germany; the confiscation of entire industrial facilities as a result of a war which ended in a stalemate; but was lost in a peace treaty. During WWII when France was defeated this point is further validated by the fact that France signed its surrender to German hands in the same rail car which the treaty of Versailles was signed in out of spite.

HISTORICAL DISTORTIONS

The reason history is distorted is to avoid taking responsibility for the results of historical injustice. The war did however take a surprising turn at the end by demonstrating the danger of overt racism and eugenics, which was practiced worldwide previously. When I look at WWII it has the same emotional response to my generation, as the generation that fought in WWII must have felt towards the Napoleonic wars. This is a battle of my grandparents; the stuff of history. There are still people alive who lived through that experience and their response is often emotional. They present propaganda as truth; his is why historical perspectives are never accurate until several generations later. To separate the emotion, from the experience requires an observer status, only time provides perspective. WWII never occurred in my analysis, the appropriate term should be; "The European Domination Wars" part one & part two. The two world wars as they are called are inextricably linked as one being the point of contention, leading up to the other. Should you ask the average person about World War One, the most common response is that they know little about it. How can any perspective or knowledgeable opinion be formed without this knowledge of the events leading up to the occurrence? A simple review of the speeches of Hitler clearly demonstrates that the peace treaty of World War One was used frequently to rile up the German people and was used politically to justify WWII, by the German Government, yet this perspective is seldom mentioned; a very major distortion and oversight. Frequently an edited and distorted version of his speeches is presented as he riles up the people at a rally. This is to make him appear insane by editing the presentation. He is also the man responsible for Germany in the nineteen thirties being the first western country to end the great depression within its boundaries (it was called the German miracle in the 1930s). The first highway express ways were built under him, social programs were instituted, and the Volkswagen was "the people's car" promised for every citizen and many other innovations and scientific developments such as rockets, jet aircraft, drones and space travel since copied. However, he also had a very dark side in an overpowering obsessive racist ideology which if put into perspective improved the world in the end by demonstrating the evils of racism. After the war all western nations were humiliated to reform their racist policies such as racial segregation in the southern United States, and similar colonial policies for most countries granting independence to European colonies as a result of racism, became something of concern; after all look what the Nazis did.

THE HIDDEN COST OF WAR AND SAVAGERY

War is the greatest waste of mankind. I shudder to think and wonder; how many great idealists, innovators, inventions, theories, artists and promoters of human progress have been killed in the thousands of battles throughout history? How about the witch hunts of the middle ages or the Spanish Inquisition? How many millions of plain good people were killed in the former Soviet Union by wrong-headed Social engineering because their ideas were unacceptable to the communist establishment; it is estimated that millions of people more were killed in the former Soviet Union in their gulags and in the Ukraine from brutal land theft resulting in starvation, than in the holocaust. How many Armenians (In Turkey) which was a model for Hitler's Holocaust to exterminate the Jews, or other minorities in other countries such as China; how about the killing fields of Cambodia in recent decades? Perhaps one of those who were killed was an Einstein? Imagine how different the world might be if Einstein were killed in the Holocaust, perhaps no nuclear knowledge or theory of relativity? Has our science exceeded our social development because the philosophers were killed in battle, or persecuted and sent to some gulag to die? Our evolution as a society has been hindered to a level we can only speculate. Did all this provide a lesson overriding these human losses, by providing and education regarding prejudice, which makes it all worth the loss? Did we get something out of it to improve the human condition? Did we learn to fear war so much that "mutually assured destruction" is the final notice to mankind to smarten up or go extinct by our own reckless hands? Segregation was eliminated in the United States within two decades after the war, and later South Africa was sanctioned to make reforms. However recent events in the former Yugoslavia (racial cleansing), Rwanda, and elsewhere reveal that the beast is still with us and the Middle East is ripe with religious prejudice and persecution. So, the world continues with these power plays. The battle for domination to minimize competition in trade continues. Perhaps our messiah (Socrates or like-minded person) was killed, and the crossroad we took in the past will kill our species in the end or another possibility is; What if the future dictator Adolph Hitler was eliminated by assassination, prior to the war? The answer to these speculations we will never know. However, to waste the lessons of history is the greatest waste of the human generations lost.

THE LEARNING CURVE OF HUMANITY

We are apprentices who refuse to learn from our past mistakes. We must become properly educated to improve our world and stop history from repeating its mistakes. The contemporary perspective of an edited history is similar to entering a room in the middle of an argument, not knowing what started it, but when you enter you observe one person beating on another. The natural reaction is a desire to intervene and tell the person of violence to "get a grip on yourself"; to stop behaving in such an outrageous fashion. If the violent person kills someone s/he is legally charged as a murderer. Often it is said that; "that person deserves the death penalty", however soldiers killing is ok. This is where most perspectives stop, with an opinion of limited knowledge. The matter goes to a court of law; the "murderer" tells a sad story. The person murdered has; "raped and killed, his wife and children". Due to this information, you now feel compassion towards the murderer. The brute is not a brute, but rather a sick outraged victim. The entire situation is now completely different. What happened to change your perspective? Murder is illegal, killing another person on the orders of your Government in circumstances of war is all right? But you cannot do that regardless of the injustice to your family. The state can be violent and use teargas and water cannon, bats and guns on unarmed civilians to end protest. But the citizen is guilty of assault if he tried the same thing on his own behalf – Is this justice or hypocrisy? This is an example of Social engineering, propaganda by Government, to indoctrinate citizens. Propaganda is the presentation of partial truth ignoring the complete picture. Without full perspective of history, we know only a partial distorted picture of the circumstances of our everyday existence. Propaganda takes an incident and pulls it out of context. By misquoting reality, to cover up societies own guilt, certain aspects are not revealed. Propaganda prevents justice from ever occurring, the root causes of problems are never dealt with. We only speak the truth when we review history in the distant future. Real history is seldom written until the participants die, the truth is recorded by subsequent generations. Scholars who have an interest in the topic are the few people who realize these things. Therefore, by applying the new altered values and knowledge to the study of the past, our previous interpretation is often found to be false. Unless we apply the perspective of the era in which the activities occurred, to the recount of history and recognize that hindsight in seeing the whole picture, changes our perspective. We now know what the participants could never know; the truth, only hindsight is 20/20. I do not state this as a put down or justifications of say the Second World War or anything which occurred in the past. This is however an excellent example of how history can only be interpreted with perspective of time. The present; even in our current time frame, we have no concept of the true big picture regarding current affairs. What secrets the politician's hide or the media does not report or falsely reports and cover up to get us worked up into a frenzy. Where does the seed of truth begin and the lies end? The majority never knows, we often trust others who have agendas and vested interest never revealed until time passes. History is the only judge of today's actions, which is legitimate. Unfortunately, the past is often distorted in popular culture and used as a means to achieve moral dominance, to create subjugation and entrenchment of power and authority. This is to the detriment of the benefits history can offer as an education for the improvement of the human condition. History often reveals the truth; truths of propaganda, truths of deception, truths of timely secrets, finally revealed. Incompetence, stupidity and mismanagement all these things which are the lessons of history. History is a bitter pill particularly if someone you care about suffers or dies as a result of any of these actions; so, coverups occur, to protect the guilty. The truth can never be told other than to future generations. Future generations are negligent in using history lessons due to indifference. Lack of personal involvement even in circumstances a generation into the future makes a big difference to human reactions. Abuse and loss of human life without justified purpose continues. The variables are shaken up like a salad dressing and it all continues generation after generation; with the same result. The sad part is that generations of human beings cannot pass on knowledge genetically for we have no prior knowledge. If we did the world would be a much more peaceful place; hundreds, perhaps thousands of years ago. Perhaps we are criminals of complacency towards our past? Perhaps we are wise to forget the past least we continue old animosities? Perhaps we should keep the past in perspective with the times, without complacency or animosities, least we are negligent of the lesson for which our ancestors paid for with their lives.

COMPLACENCY

Complacency, with history, with current affairs, this is the state of most western nations. Only when matters affect people personally do they really give a dam. Negligence from one generation to the next is why we use the old expression; "History repeats itself". Is this a world of sheep, fools or indifference? The society of do-nothing observers, spectators, or simply cowards or are we simply complicit? The common person expresses impotence, but are they impotent or are we all accessories because we do nothing? We leave the demise of others under circumstances of injustice in isolated struggles. The beneficiary of those who fight however is often the indifferent observer. How can s/he claim the right to be a beneficiary of someone else's pain and hardship without guilt? Do we not aid injustice by not becoming involved? Isn't indifference permission & co-operation? Oh yes we are often angered by current affairs which we feel are unjust. But does anger remove our accessory status? Though it is common practice to blame Politicians, Lawyers, Judges, the system and many others for the injustices of society. I ask, where is the integrity of the common person? Also, we are so lacking that our status is a spectator of the television of reality. A Coliseum of modern society, watching spectacles of injustice and finding it only entertaining. We are no different than the Romans watching the murder and harm of innocents in the Coliseum for entertainment.

The fundamental inadequacy is a lack of historical and social education by the majority, who are delinquent of all responsibility. It is far easier to claim an inability to do anything than to even write a simple letter of objection or protest, even a few pennies for a postage stamp to note a protest is too much to expect it seems. This clearly demonstrates a lack of historical and social   evolution by the vast majority of people and an irresponsible nature. We live in a world of social illiterates of our collective social   and historical foundations. The average citizen has no opinions and must listen to the radio or watch the television to get one so as to mouth someone else's slant on a circumstance. All media are reactionary by nature, they have a perspective of immediacy rather than histories where realities leading up to a particular circumstance commenced. My experience is that the average person does not have an opinion, if the media does not give them one! The very concept of criminal complacency is offensive to the western mind. The average citizen lives under the illusion of innocence as a spectator. But doesn't the spectator lend support and legitimacy to the event and process as it occurs by not speaking up at least? This mass ignorance can only be excused by stating that a lack of understanding by the majority, a lack of education, and perspective with respect to social responsibility is the problem. Perhaps preoccupation with their own economic survival is the best that can be done; am I being too harsh?

Our jails are full of innocent people; it is just the evidence or plea bargaining (often admitting to crimes not committed) which put them there. Few of them feel they deserve to be in jail, for in their own minds and opinions they did nothing wrong. If they felt they did wrong wouldn't they all confess and request the penalty, seldom does this happen in reality? Most Mothers feel their child could never do such a thing, however mothers usually live in ignorance & extreme bias. One could call pre-meditated murder a lack of conscience, is it self-justified ignorance or vigilante violence? When is vigilante violence justified in an unjust world? But whose ignorance it is depends upon the circumstance of the crime. Society of course is never to blame, and the guilty party always has rights in most western societies; but not the victim. The criminal often has a sad tale to tell of abuse or poverty. Somehow the tale must be modified by defence lawyers, to create such a story to create empathy. The criminal gets free legal representation at the expense of the taxpayer, often s/he is railroaded to a false plea bargain to make the prosecution's lack of evidence an easier prosecution. The cost of the system gets in the way of honest determination. The issue of criminal guilt is a complicated one, because each case has different circumstance. For those who claim to be mentally ill, psychology is so imprecise that it is still more in the realm of philosophical speculation rather than science, though recent developments, and magnetic resonance imaging scanning technology is providing enlightenment. Vested interest basically sums up the corruption of the system of today which villainizes without bases in fact and analysis. Essentially guilt for the ways of the world, is carried on all our shoulders as participants and as witnesses of corruption we all carry guilt; though we deny it. Our responsibility is to be informed, and to inform how actions in sequence effects everything. Everything in life is exchange, cooperation and collaboration. One person cannot change the world, however many doing a lot of small things does add up to a great improvement; complacency is consent.

GUIDELINES FOR THE SOCIAL ENGINEERS PERSPECTIVE

It is a common practice under politically correct ideology for corporate, Government agenda's and interest groups; to initiate distortions, slants, false interpretations and otherwise attempt to alter the historical record and other realities to appropriate an individual or groups purposes and agenda. Often interest groups will encourage or create distortions of the truth for power; to enhance the truth of record, to make it more dramatic and influential; thus, creating a state of sympathy for the cause. Deception by authorities is commonly accepted as truth by the people who do not have the background or time to research the issues for themselves. I present this perspective to illustrate the danger of ignorance and the abuses which take place through lies and deception, for no other reason than power over others by the purveyors of lies, which currently is a very common human activity. If a person has the right to an opinion, then that perspective carries the obligation to become informed, to see the truth. Thus, the Social Engineer must not only know history, but also analyse and see history, economics and other problems from a perspective of all other available sources. Reviewing the intention of legislation and the resulting outcome to ensure harmony. Social Engineers need to organize this analysis in charts to clarify the results in point form and clarify these things the following are required:

1. UNDERSTAND; the intention of the law and policy or regulation.

2. UNDERSTAND; the circumstance that leads up to the regulation or policy.

3. ANALYSE; the implementation and how it was or will be implemented.

4. REVIEW AND STUDY; the outcome in terms of actual effects in pragmatic terms, by searching for similar circumstance in history.

5. PREDICT WITH AVAILABLE KNOWLEDGE; the sociological effects in terms of foreseeable behavioural outcomes.

6. REVIEW AND CHART; the negative and positive effects regarding what and how policy was implemented.

7. DETERMINE; the modifications necessary to correct negative effects and pursue the positive.

8. ADVOCATE AND DOCUMENT; the justification for modification via examples of outcomes.

9. HAVE A MACRO UNDERSTANDING; in order to create; a summary and conclusion, based upon pragmatic reality.

10. THE COURT OF SOCIAL ENGINEERING; should be its practitioners via peer review, reviewing the analysis reports of each other and maintaining high standards of ethics.

11. UTILIZING METHODOLOGIES; corresponding to analysis utilizing, "applied project management" techniques that creates sequential analysis utilizing historical precedents.

12. DOCUMENT ORIGINAL INTENTIONS AND OUTCOMES; that get placed into the summary of analysis. Utilizing "bibliometrics," to expand the social engineer's topical comprehension of society's activities, in order to formulate comprehensive analysis.

13. SOCIAL ENGINEERING REPORTS NEED TO BE COMPREHENSIVE AND ORGANIZED; with comprehensive easy to see indexed tabs; comparative; conclusions and analysis, the means to rectify social , political and other policy to be beneficially modified, eliminated or implemented as a conclusion in their reports, which should be available to all stake holders.

14. WHO, WHAT, WHERE, WHEN AND WHY; Just like an impartial journalist, the social engineer must supply a complete historical perspective and utilize social and scientific psychological information, as it is available in all analysis without bias or favouritism.

15. THE SOCIAL ENGINEER MUST BE ETHICAL; and I believe there must be an accreditation process along with certifications at the college and or University level of study.

16. EDUCATIONAL DEPARTMENTS; for the bibliometric study and peer review of Social Engineer's pre-analyse of laws, policies and revolution to determine sequential outcomes based upon analysis of all fields study that are interrelated; thus, law will be implemented with functional pragmatic outcomes, in such a manner as to enable the benefits of historical experience of humanity inuring to the future for the benefit of society.

17. PROPERLY TRAINED SOCIAL ENGINEERS WOULD BE

EMPLOYED; by Government, corporations and institutions, to implement more successful policy and other initiatives based upon charted facts, and pre-analysis; to create an ethical and pragmatic social architecture that respects the individual.

18. APPLIED PROJECT MANAGEMENT; will be transformed to a new type of project management that is oriented to Social engineering; by a revised methodology of systemization to create standardized methodologies. Determined by universal ethics as outline in this book. Social engineering and analysis will determine performance criteria and accreditation for the profession's field of endeavour.

19. UNIVERSAL ETHICS; are the macro perspective of authentic vested interest, to the greatest number of people, respecting the individual and society's acceptance of: The rights of one as being the rights and benefits of all in equal application. Thus, the maintenance of justice is; implemented without benefit to vested interest and its corrupting influence. This does not equate equality of outcome ! It's equality of treatment and opportunity.

Chapter 6

MIND OVER HUMAN NATURE

I t is important for the Social Engineer to comprehend the fundamentals of human nature. The human species is an egocentric creature from conception. When we are born our awareness of the world commences with an awareness of ourselves. First; of the physical nature of our existence. Then of the not only physical, but also the psychological separateness of ourselves from the world that surrounds us. Know thyself is a fundamental lesson we must all learn. Our dependency upon physical elements causes human perspectives to often be short sighted do to our limited linear perceptions. Within our life's everything in this physical existence has a definite beginning and end, this is linear existence. We are creatures of four dimensions, Height, width & depth not to mention one other important aspect, duration (time). The following is a sequential presentation of human behavioural development:

A: QUESTIONS OF INFANCY:
- What am I?
- Who am I?
- What are these other beings?
- Am I one of them?
- Where am I?
- What are these (i.e. hands)?

B: INFANT ACQUIRES ANSWERS:
- They are not me.

- I am separate.
- What will they allow me to do?
- What can I do?
- What are the limitations, are there any?
- How do I do this?

C: EGOTISM:

Gradually in progressive steps the ego incrementally grows to become a being that becomes increasingly seemingly independent. Perceptions of limitations of self-growth only become accepted with age. Gradually for most people other than the antisocial (mentally ill), time and experience teaches the need to enlist the co-operation of others by trade. This desire arises out of the wish to fulfil individual wants, needs and desires. The need to enlist the co-operation of others arises out of the realisation that others have abilities resources and skills which the egocentric self lacks.

D: AGE PROGRESSION:

When we get older concerns of limitations and ability are replaced by concerns of purpose.

- What is this life all about?
- Why am I here?
- What is right, and what is wrong?
- What is the truth?
- What would happen if?
- How much time do I have?

PRINCIPAL CHARACTERISTICS OF HUMAN NATURE:

Let's deal with these issues one at a time. The human species is ego-centric, meaning we inaccurately see ourselves as the centre of all existence, our thought process asks constantly, how this experience (all experiences) relate back to me. This method of thinking is the downfall of human society.

1. The human species is myopic with respect to the consequences of our actions. We do harm to each other without regard to the implications, as we lack a macro

perspective.

2. The human species is an exchange-oriented creature by necessity, even that which often appears to be altruistic is motivated by egocentric attitudes and exchange. Religion often brings forth altruistic behaviours in an attempt to appease your God or fraternity of like-minded individuals; which is an indoctrinated individual perceived salvation.

3. Our perceptions commence with our natural characteristics; which is the foundation our consciousness is built upon. These characteristics; are developed as a result of personal experience and by our level and kind of education. We are not a complete "Tabula-rasa". Like all creatures, we are born with a survival foundation of behavioural unconscious instinctive knowledge, and inherited characteristics; that are behavioural. It is absurd to think that we only inherit physical appearances from our ancestors; as though there is some definitive limit to the inherited characteristics in humanity. Given no other species including ourselves demonstrate any such behavioural separation in the nature of all species.

4. People are self-deceiving, delude themselves and others; concerning their behaviour, misleading others that selfish desires are altruistic. Altruism is a characteristic necessary to protect off-spring and in the macro of society implements initiatives for the benefit of progeny and group cohesion. Otherwise humanity would suffer from, excessive narcissistic behaviour; excessive environmental exploitation without a care.

5. We learn that reciprocity and exchange must occur at some point, or discontent will result; thus, it is prudent to perceive our pragmatic limits to fulfil our desires. Ego-centrism we learn if we are astute is linear, and thus

returns to us if our thinking does not evolve to become wholistic to encourage trade.

These behaviours are instinct for the human being and are required for survival upon an often-hostile planet. Human ideas of life and physical existence is a perceived reality regulated by perceptions and experiential perspective. Human egocentric behaviour by its very nature is often crude. This behaviour begins at birth with the demands we make as a baby for attention nourishment and care of the self. The cry of the baby is the announcement to the world; "I am here I have needs take care of me -NOW!"

There are two basic motivations of the human being: The fear of loss and the desire for gain. Think about these motivations the next time you buy something or do some form of work in your personal life, which one is your motivation? Questioning if they are right or wrong, is not an appropriate philosophical question, since these are fundamental behavioural characteristics of the human species and prehistoric instincts for survival. The pursuit of egocentric desires using these motivations is reflected back to us like a mirror of our lives everything we do is mirrored back to us; in repercussions.

NATURAL FUNDAMENTALS

The basic rule is the ancient "Golden Rule"; "Do onto others as you would have them do unto you"; because they eventually will. Breaking this code of nature is not without consequences; the boomerang effect (law of return) takes place when natural rules are broken. Dishonest people relate to other persons who are dishonest and so have this behaviour returned to them. Only a thief will relate to a thief and therefore the thief will be stolen from. The parallels are many and a fundamental reality of life; others will do onto you as you do onto others. Biblical: " An eye for an eye, a tooth for a tooth".

The evidence of this is an everyday aspect of our lives. The primary evidence of this is the" natural law of return" (Our lives are interconnected in a fractal circle). What you put out will return to you; put out good and positive actions and energy; good will return to you; put out negative actions and energy; and negative actions will return to you. This all sounds very metaphysical however experience has demonstrated to me that it is accurate and not based upon superstition, as I will explain the bases of this further; later herein along with the foundational and philosophical bases of natural law. Wealth, health, and survival is a human concern and natural law also affects its success or failure. Social engineering often undermines this process of natural law and makes things worse; as interloping always carries ramifications.

1. Natural law functions by its "code of ramifications" with indifference to human physical perceptions.

2. Natural law only provides that you reap what you sow; this is balance.

3. The ego central self within all people is powerful because it gives all individuals complimentary talents and abilities, that if utilised in balance; without threat or forced domination are good for all as items of trade.

4. The dominance of one person over another diminishes the dominated person and is contrary to the arrogance of the ego, upsets balance and will result in rebellion eventually.

INNER VOICES

Science has recently uncovered that, there are fundamentally three major types of thinkers, not everyone has an inner monologue. This is a relatively new discovery in brain science. There are:

1. Verbal thinkers: Verbal thinkers think in words or whole sentences.

2. **Pattern thinkers:** Think in patterns and connections; thinking in actions and emotions.
3. **Visual thinkers:** Think in pictures and images.

Many people are a combination of all three. The implications of this are yet to be fully comprehended. Clearly individuality is far more comprehensive than previously thought, as we even think in different terms, utilizing different thought processes.

HUMAN PERSPECTIVES

There are four natural characteristic types of wo/men in the world:

1. The materialist.
2. The idealist.
3. The escapist.
4. A predatory nature.

The Materialists

Have dominated the past two centuries, constituting the establishment, their focus in life is for material gain; often without concern for natural law; acting purely out of self-interested rationalization. This is lineal thought and explains why we are one of a series of collapsed civilizations, Human civilization will always come to an end with societies that indulge lineal development; because it is a path to social , environmental and political decay due to the accumulation of ramifications caused by short term thinking.

The Idealists

Idealists are commonly creative intellectual individuals. Sometimes followers of religious faith, and political or philosophical agendas. The idealist has faith in something beyond material gain for abstract reasons and rationality.

The Escapist

Escapists feel alienated from society go beyond independent thinking into a separate life and consciousness, in that they do not fit in as they are usually cognitively detached from others and can end up; mentally ill, alcohol or drug addicted, sometimes a hermit or living on the streets. They are self-perpetu-ating of a myriad of problems for themselves. They are self-jus-tifying and self-indulgent; our jails are filled with them. These behaviours can dominate a personality, we can be a mix of these personality types to varying degrees.

Predators

The human species has a solitary predatory aspect to our na-tures which manifests more in some individuals than others, which we also call psychopathy. These are very dangerous self-indulgent individuals. They abuse and deceive others for in-dividual benefit and have typically an undeveloped brain pre-frontal lobe. When they see weakness in others for self-eco-nomic advantage, they manipulate circumstances for personal advantage.

This creates great social angst and often trauma. Only empathy keeps nature in check as it is the product of experience. Child-hood trauma causes a great deal of lifetime hinderances in many people. There are presently many elites with this mental handi-cap.

EVOLUTION

There is no denying that natural selection occurs, however it may only be advantage gained by circumstance. Charles Darwin wrote in "The Origin of the Species and The descent of Man;" theories about the origins of species and human evolution. The twists and lies attached to those writings by organised religion, business and the half educated, who never read the book, are for the most part misrepresentations. The following are common misrepresentations of the theories of Charles Darwin:

1. That Darwin claimed; "That people descended from monkeys." Darwin actually stated that people perhaps descended from lower or ape like creatures; not mon-keys. Besides it was a scientific theory, not gospel and subject to revision as our anthropological and biological

knowledge increases.

2. Charles Darwin stated that nature advances via the means of; "natural selection". Darwin stated that this process of natural selection occurs via variation. That the fittest could be any variable; from plumage (looks); physical power (strength); intelligence; or other advantage, such as ability to run or fly away from your adversaries or obtain other advantage. In some instances, it could be economic, or the most prolific breeder. "The origin of the species" is a book concerning biology.

3. Darwin's theories of biological evolution were never a justification for cut throat business behaviour; or had anything to do with either business or human social constructs. Human business economics and trade have nothing to do with it, stating this is a distortion of the realities of the theory of evolution.

4. "Survival of the fittest" was an idea propagated by the separate philosophical concepts of Herbert Spencer's philosophy. While Darwin the biologist, touted a process called; "Natural Selection;" in his scientific work, based upon the study of nature.

5. Darwin's ideas are often confused with the philosophy of Herbert Spencer who coined the terms: "Survival of the fittest" and "Evolution;" prior to Darwin publishing his studies in his book.

6. The process of "Natural Selection" as referred to under Darwinian perspective is very different from Herbert Spencer's philosophy, presenting his opinions. Verses Charles Darwin's scientific studies and voyages on board the HMS Beagle which gave Darwin a scientifically observable base, for his theory of "natural selection".

7. A correlation can be made to accuse Herbert Spencer

as being the father to Nazi ideology, in that it is the expected sequence one would anticipate from those adopting the philosophy of Herbert Spencer starting with eugenics; and many other
horrors of the twentieth century including what we now call the holocaust in Nazi Germany. Spenser clearly had many psychopathic characteristics.

8. Spencer was known in his time to have a brutal attitude towards the poor and disadvantaged and had little empathy for others. Herbert Spencer's philosophy is one that demonstrates strong psychopathic cognitive development in him; and those who espouse his brutal ideas; that have a very callous attitude towards human relationships; human society; evolution; trade; and little comprehension of the necessity for integrity as the foundations of long-term business relationships and trade.

9. Spencer did not seem to comprehend the human desire for exchange, and the importance of integrity in business. Spencer's philosophical social   perspectives demonstrate an ideology that is brutal and lacking empathy and compassion for others and is ruthless. Characteristics for which he was well known, as having a brutal lack of empathy or compassion for others in his lifetime.

10. Spencer grew up under brutal circumstances and does not seem to comprehend that long-term business relations are built upon fair and equitable trade and commerce; rather than brutal exploitation of advantage. In the long term this behaviour would have disastrous business results, and sway others away from conducting business with a person so ruthless.

COMMUNISM & EVOLUTIONARY CHANGES IN THOUGHT

The Communistic regimes of the post-World War One 1917 era demonstrated that human initiative is necessary; and that communal hierarchy and material equality removed incentive. The Soviet Communists found this out very quickly and created a party-based ideology imposing a different class system, for a supposedly egalitarian classless society as communist theory would assert. The human ego needs incentive to take initiative; the examples are infinite, perhaps the post WWII cold war demonstrated it best; that free enterprise economies with free people, where human rights are respected flourish. While Chinese and Soviet era communists copied the creations and innovations of free nations because communist economies are lethargic due to a lack of any initiative, their political and legal system creates. Only when people are free does creativity and initiative flourish. The same holds true for China under its current totalitarian Government regime, which was and is; the transference of western production to take advantage of minimal labour protections and environmental protections; to increase corporate profits and reduce market costs, in our current era. Communism as an ideology came out of the early industrial revolution, and is in practice at present in China, it duplicates the brutality of European industry at the dawn of the industrial revolution, hypocritically under state control. Communism lacks innovation without individual motive or incentive, thus it failed pragmatically as an economic and social   system by being a totalitarian form of Government as it has to build walls to cage in their people from their desire to escape and leave the repression of ambition. Though China unlike the former East Bloc Soviet society is so over populated, as to have no need to prevent their population from migrating to other nations at present, as migration is like a pressure relief valve allowing malcontents to go away voluntarily and makes pretence of being a nation with liberty. Class based exploiting workers was criticised by Karl Marx and was his justification for a communist revolution. What it pragmatically creates is a hierarchy based upon affiliation with the communist party system, as in reality without hierarchy society reverts to chaos.

In recent decades western corporations have moved entire industries to China, and thus reducing the costs of production, in keeping with the kind of ideology that Herbert Spencer would advocate under his philosophical ideas. Costs of production for consumer goods, in the unregulated Chinese market has been greatly decreased; causing in China an extra ordinary level of environmental pollution and degradation, including foul air and causing cancer afflicting the Chinese people in their cities in ever increasing numbers. Exploiting human resources; so as to treat human beings as utilitarian objects and discarding injured workers as though they are refuse is a common practice in China at present; as is slave prison labour of various types. Which is also presently practiced in the United States with prisoners in many prisons. Great strides have been made in lifting many Chinese poor out of poverty, with imported western industry. Repression of natural human behaviours in trade, by collectivizing their society to the point of reaching a collapse occurred in the former Soviet Union in their failed experiment with communism. Hundreds of millions of people have paid for this ideology in what has been the most blood-soaked century we know of in human history as a result of this failed ideology in brutal murders by their own government's hands. Under this ideology in China and the defunct Soviet Union. In the former Soviet Union, Ukrainian and other farmers suffered from an unjust farm and land distribution system of theft, and murder in gulags; of slave labour for political dissidents, under brutal conditions. Communism is an economic ideology that has proven to be an unmitigated failure, often reliant upon grain imports from western nations to prevent mass starvation. Similar land distribution policies have impoverished Zimbabwe in Africa and are presently being exercised in South Africa with the same murderous results and agricultural collapse. Communists never seem to learn from their historical failures. Blinded by their utopia delusion.

Trade leads to a more humane free enterprise system in a non-repressive and democratically free society as in America, and Western Europe at present to a lesser degree. The strength of the free enterprise system is derived from self-interested competition forcing innovation. This accelerates technological evolution to improve society's quality of material life at a much more rapid pace than central planning has ever been able to achieve in recorded history. The world is now very developed, industrial ability to create weapons of war is now too democratized. We must revise our views concerning world trade, to only allow free trade amongst equals in terms of environmental and workers' rights, otherwise opening up trade with countries such as China, creates an unbalanced trading ground that is exploitive in so many ways of Chinese workers, and polluting the environment, that they do by repressing all dissent.

Political instability will most definitely become an issue in China, as in the former Soviet Union, unless the Chinese Government can and does implement the needed reform. Clearly there are efforts to improve the situation in China, because it appears that in event of a recession there is a strong likelihood that mass political unrest will come from the exploitation; from raising expectations; from the Chinese people. Thus, such business practices such as globalism is only of temporary benefit, because such a situation eventually creates a great deal of social animosity amongst the people as an aspect of human nature, leading eventually to social unrest. Having an equal field of trade is exploitive and has many unintended consequences that have not been considered, as it is a form of corporate colonialism.

Abraham Maslow's hierarchy of needs is a better model in terms of understanding human motivations. Humane development needs to be made a priority due to human nature in order to have social harmony. Human society is never stagnant; thus, we can expect constant change as being normal. The fundamental codes of human behaviour are revealed in nature; these are:

1. **Know thyself and you will know right from wrong.** Informed consent is fundamental for righteousness and maintaining peace.

2. The person without conscience has no excuse for harming others; because everyone is aware of how they themselves do not and would not like to be treated.

3. When a wrong or good behaviour is implemented, a cycle is created which will return to the society and the social engineer can chart the outcome that results. Human nature returns an injustice for an injustice and good for good. What you spread will return to society.

4. Life parallels a person walking undefended into a wild lion cage. The expected outcome is dinner time for the lion, and death to the person. Actions equal conclusions; simple example!

THE SOCIAL ENGINEERS PERSPECTIVE

Because of the human being's ability to think far beyond instinct we are the only creatures on the earth that can create unnatural cycles. When we interfere with nature we usually poison or harm ourselves; behaviour returns in a natural cycle. The ancient rule of "Do unto others as you would have them do unto you "has its implications beyond common thought. What you put out will return to you. Natural rules about life are:

1. You are born with a physical body, you will die one day like all the plants animals and other living things which have proceeded you.

2. There is the natural cycle as such everything in the material realm obeys this law: Physical life is finite. Disobedience in human constructs destroys their ability to endure if they do not follow these rules.

3. We are here to fulfil our cycle on earth (birth, childhood, teen years, maturity, old age and death) nature demonstrates this, when it is completed, we proceed into the next cycle; decomposition and possibly a spiritual existence that cannot be absolutely ruled out as there is no way to prove the opposite at this time in human scientific enquiry.

4. Everything including actions proceeds to a conclusion that is foreseeable with proper analysis of the nature of processes, and natural behaviour. The Social Engineer must gear his analysis to scientific determinations of the natural entropy of action to reveal the outcome by forecasting the likely result by pre-forensic study.

NATURE'S ENERGY

Modern physics has determined our bodies are made of energy which is immortal and never dies, although it also changes and evolves (similar to the Asian concept of chi).

1. Everything is composed of energy, our bodies flow in harmony with the energy of our environment; this energy flows through us.

2. Energy exists in a wide variety of frequencies it is never destroyed it is only transformed, this is a rule of physics.

3. The Essence of nature (God to some) is an all-knowing energy that is the essence of everything. The physical is integrated into this omniscient existence. All entities and dimensional planes of existence are part of this natural realm of energy.

4. All of us are energy in a body; we have a responsibility and duty to ourselves to acquire a better understanding of the flow of this energy and its cyclical nature.

5. Everything flows in natural interconnected fractal cycles. We live in the physical material world, which is made of energy, is fluid, ever changing, and temporary; eventually all physical material dies, rots and will disintegrate providing fertilizer for the future; its energy spent and transformed. We do not have any proof if our consciousness also transfers elsewhere after our physical body's death as per many religious beliefs with any proven scientifically based verification at this time.

6. That which is physical by nature needs material amenities by necessity. Trade satisfies material need and desire.

SELF PRESERVATION

You must protect and nurture your physical and psychological self, or you will suffer hardship, be used, be abused by others, this is self-interest; it is natural and is not unethical by nature's rules. The protection of the rights of others defends your own rights by mutual protection. When attacking minorities is acceptable, we all lose our rights because you are a minority of one, and we thus all become targets. The divide and conquer principal in Government and military strategy is as old as humanity itself and continues to be used to dupe people very effectively to this very day.

RELATIVE VIEWS

We are all corrupted by the perspective determined by our life experiences and education. Where your circumstance is at this point in your development determines your perspective. This is not stationary for humans unless the person is mentally handicapped; as animals also have a limited perspective.

OUR SYMBIOTIC WORLD

Everything works by a cyclical natural energy governing the Universe, the Galaxy and the solar system; the natural processes on earth; human life and death; human behaviours. Social Engineers must understand cycles are fundamental to all analysis.

1. Should behaviour be symbiotic, positive will be returned to society.

2. These laws are unbreakable, as they are the laws of nature in the physical realm, physics also verifies this.

Truths of nature are pure, honest, self-evident, and inescapable; incorruptible, interlaced and balanced. When the balance is changed repercussions will result. The principal of physics as discovered by Sir. Isaac Newton is that, "For every action there is an equal and opposite reaction". This is a law of nature that applies to human interaction as well as the physical activities we impose upon the biosphere of the earth. Nature is a symbiotic flow of everything, we cannot escape nature; we are a part of it.

Balance
Everything must be done in balance with the natural characteristics of everything else; because the natural world exists in symbiotic balance. The scales of nature always rebound to be level; however, "level" is relative to the change you inflict.

Truth
Nature tells no lies, spreads no deceptions, and has no agenda; it simply exists in indifference; its existence is absolute and unwavering honesty. For the Social Engineer, the study of nature is the path to clear thought. Study nature and you shall see pure truth. This truth is difficult for human kind to accept for we are confused in that we are a piece of nature; but not natural like animals or plants, we are only a component. The human being is a parasite within the host of nature.

Life equals time
Your Life equals how much time you have in a physical body. The body has limitations on its term of existence. Time does not exist for nature; it is a human concept. Nature renews itself

in a cycle (Nature is infinity); therefore, in nature time is irrelevant and a human construct.

Co-operation & flow

No person is a world unto themselves. The Co-operation of others is necessary in trade and for survival. Cooperation makes life easier and provides insurance in times of difficulty. Each person's life is like a stream of water, directed in a focus of learning and exchange with others. Follow the stream as only you know where its natural limitations will lead you.

Fair play

Exchange and trade is a Long-term co-operative venture that can only succeed if all of the participants and recipients are receiving fair and relative benefit in exchange and or opportunity. Egocentricity is a primary characteristic of human nature, we must learn that the world is a macro circumstance. This does not mean we should sacrifice our self-interest, as self-interest provides a benefit to society at large in exchange for a personal reward; money or prestige to the innovator. Talent has the human right to the rewards of its capacity, to inure it's benefits to all.

Chapter 7

EVERYTHING IS INTERCONNECTED TO THE MIND

Social Engineers must understand certain fundamentals. There is an essential question of; does your life belong to you or are you owing to a series of obligations to which you do not recall committing yourself to? When I was born I do not recall any pre-obligatory agreements. The family and society in which a person is raised in childhood usually determines a person's sense of ethics, it is foundational to society! The only agreement which I can decipher is that life comes with natural agreements. Here are the fundamentals:

1. I will have no choice but to die, human beings are mortal and at a certain point in the future we all die; the date of which we all have no say. *The law of impartiality.*

2. I had no choice regarding the decision to be born; if I did, I have no recollection. *The law of determination.*

3. The only fact which I can decipher as not having a hidden human agenda, (because humanity by nature is primarily self-interested thus egocentric) with any sense of absolute trust are those aspects of life which are not man-made; the laws of nature. Nature has no vested interest to deceive anyone; therefore, it is reliable as a source of information beyond human conjecture and doctrine. *The law of vested interest.*

4. Since my birth people have been constantly trying to exploit how I should utilise my most fundamental and supreme asset; my life and the perspective I view it from. Usually this is done to benefit the establishment simply to maintain the status quo, benefit themselves and create a power base of followers. *The law of subversion.*

5. By the evidence of experience, I know that life requires I perform exchange with others to achieve a good quality life by working also. *The law of social contract.*

6. Business and Government are well aware of life's limitations, so they have created retirement as a carrot placed in front of the human donkey for motivation creating a happy face to this grim reality after age 65. *The law of motivation.*

7. Health starts to fail in old age via reduced stamina, productivity and decreased physical abilities are expected as a normal development beyond this point. The old are removed like old worn out machines because industry has no patience for the less agile and the young continually replace the old. This natural agreement of life is predetermined absolute and without previous failure to succeed. *The law of time limitation.*

8. No one that I have ever met can tell me with any certainty (barring faith - belief without physical proof) that I will ever live again. I am not seeking to harm others, I only wish to maintain and retain that which is my supreme asset; my life. I know of no person who has ever returned from the dead to tell me that it is such a great experience or for that matter anything else about death; except in myth. *The law of self-ownership of my life.*

9. Deaths experience supplies no verifiable proof to the living and has no witnesses in the living whose visions can

be scientifically proven beyond a doubt. However, as a means to control others the idea of a afterlife can and has been successfully manipulated. I say all this to point out that life is precious; -all life! No concrete evidence of an afterlife other than faith has ever been provided. Perhaps the concept of an afterlife was created to make me not feel exploited in letting other people use my life to their selfish ends and create a hierarchy, wealth and a comfortable life for themselves; seeking to create my acquiescence. Everywhere I look I see humans using and controlling others for their own purposes. I see deception on a grand scale, people using others to advance their self-interest with material riches. *The law of vested interest.*

10. The necessity of trade and competition demonstrates that no person is a self-contained Island; we are all interdependent working for the acquisition of the necessities of life this is an indisputable reality. *The law of interdependence and trade.*

11. The human ego knows no limits and is excessive in its preoccupation with aggrandizing itself, human beings are a collection of egos wanting to be god, or at minimum a god in a fiefdom. The kingdom of the ego is the family, fellow employees, business, religion and Government; -the pecking order. Your position in the pecking order of society shall determine regarding how much food, shelter, clothing, and luxuries you acquire. "Power corrupts, and absolute power corrupts absolutely" goes the old saying. The hunger for power is a fundamental aspect of human nature to control trade I have observed. Like raw milk settling; so does the human being settle into socio-economic layers. *The law of hierarchy and human egotism.*

WHAT IS NATURAL LAW?

There is such a thing as rules of Nature; thus, we can extrapolate this as Natural Law as I have above; We cannot dispute these laws and their validity; laws regarding procreation, family, relationships etc. This provides an ethical and moral fabric to guide you in your life; it is evident to all who wish to see it by careful unbiased study of nature. The truth is apparent it has never been a mystery. I have concluded after much contemplation that Natural Law exists. That this form of law is transparent to all and is indisputably self-evident in order to be valid. To be natural law, the hand of humanity must not be able to alter it as it is self-evident. Most law imposed upon society is written, created; almost exclusively by legislators, priests or scholars. To be natural law, the hand of humanity must not be able to alter it; it must be self-evident.

Natural law is quite different as it is at the disposal to all from the least to the most educated, and the ramifications must be consistent without contradiction and apparent. All creatures in nature have a birth right to be provided with equal access to the inalienable human right to knowledge of the Essence and purpose of our being along with the ability to comprehend the ramifications. Which leaves this concept the necessity to go deeper into these waters. A random, unorganized universe would be proof of these natural laws' nonexistence. Because the universe is orderly by nature, and this has been scientifically validated, the reality of pattern creation from a singularity of thought, in an evolutionary process is conceivable and evidently proven by science. The concept of an unjust creator is inconceivable; as the singularity would be the Essence of the universe we refer to as God. Greater interpretation and definition of the singularity as it is called in astrophysics will follow. The singularity is in fact consciousness. On earth each time a child is born another consciousness comes forth. Natural Law may be indifferent, but because a universal consciousness exists, being unjust would be a contradiction to the order of all that exists in nature, that everything is designed to follow a determined order. If this law were not apparent, then there would not be a natural law of the Essence (also referred to as God). Natural law exists in all creation, as a consequence; or the expression "law" would be a contradiction of terms; for there to be law, there must be enforcement; which is a consequence, thus repercussions for avoidance or disobedience. Manmade laws are the same in that they can exist, but if not enforced immediately; they still exist. The relationship between Natural Law and the individual is both private and a personal relationship we have. Revelation is expressed by consequences, it does not have to be immediately visible, only apparent. It cannot be compromised by mankind without repercussions; or it would be fantasy. The explanations of life, its purpose, laws to live by, and Natural Law to be verified as truly valid must comply with the following:

1. Have an influence on all earthly creatures and affect our planet consistently. Be physically and scientifically verifiable in the short and long term to have this effect described.

2. Be consistent, everywhere and self-evident; though these laws can be written to explain them but need not necessarily be written; except in the case of human comprehension.

3. Regardless of how humans twist the truth it is always visible even in our contradictions, deceptions and lies as verifiably valid and thus true. Truth being consistency.

To be validated; the laws and rules of Natural Law must be unbreakable and repercussions for disobedience in the long or short term must occur. In order to be a law
or a rule, enforcement must take place. This enforcement occurs as repercussions in balance as is the natural symbiotic cycle of return; a primary rule of Natural Law. On a planet that is self-contained and cyclical in every aspect of its natural

processes; there is something very fundamental going on here, extenuating beyond our micro human perspective of the individual. This theme I assure you the reader is a building process, through which I must take you in steps.

OBSERVATIONS OF LAW ENFORCEMENT AND PERSPECTIVE

1. Faith is often the residence of deception; when only faith is required, evidence is often non-existent ("wolves in sheep's clothing"; is a biblical reference applicable). The proof of the "Essence" that has determined "Natural Law" is all that you see in the universe which exists and operates in order; and by rules I define as "natural laws". How we can determine our ethics in the order of the universe, is by understanding the processes of nature that applies to all living creatures; and things upon this planet. We cannot possibly be exempt from these rules; and repercussions must emanate from their violation upon the human condition. LAW: Pollute the stream, kill the fish; have no fish for food or clean water to drink.

2. Humans are egotistical and need to understand, as they are often deluded and or deceptive in their self-justifications; not fully understanding nature or ignoring it for their own disadvantage. Though the repercussions are eternal in their implementation, even if it is not apparent at first; because cause and effect can take time to manifest the repercussions. LAW: Domination achieves compliance but never acquiescence.

3. A fully developed pre-frontal lobe does not occur prior to our mid 20s in age, this is necessary for more broad-spectrum perspectives on life and can be cited to validate early society's veneration of elders as a source of wisdom. Wisdom in fact may be a fully developed prefrontal lobe; located were some cultures call; "The third eye"

coincidently or perhaps not. LAW: Big picture thinking comes from physical age development.

4. The written word is often used for deceptive indoctrination. Deception is a common practice and motivation for the art of twisting the truth, due to its inability to explain itself and clarify points; the irony is that I am writing this. LAW: Actions speak louder than words.

5. Like all manufacturers this "Essence" concerning natural law must have provided an owner's manual, why must faith be necessary? The truth must be self-evident to all without favouritism. Wouldn't the manufacturer produce the manual himself to maintain accuracy and prevent different interpretations as well as different worshipers, or simple misunderstanding? LAW: Repercussions are the psychopath's enemy against short term thinking.

The validity of the repercussions of natural law, is the enforcement of these laws pragmatically; to be a "law" is to have repercussions. There is clearly natural law and man-made law. The foundation of law is that it is enforced, not that it exists. The method of enforcement is inconsequential.

1. Natural Law has no specific intentions for the human being in laying down the law. These laws are in every tree, plant, animal and person and only benefit from the written or spoken word to explain reality; reality is natural law's domain. Natural law is supreme in that being circular laws damages afflict humanity as consequences, by the law of return from living in an enclosed environment.

2. The Essence via natural law managed to create all that exists without humans; therefore, I am confident that natural law is not different. I am also confident that any mythological God, Essence and or natural law would let

something as ego-centrically biased as the human being be the middle man and control the doctrine. However, I expect an arrogant human being to delude its self-regarding it's superiority over the entirety of its environment in cognitive dissonance.

3. Natural law is all around, and apparent to all in nature; via comprehension of natural processes and how they operate scientifically. Humans are part of the natural order; neither above or below in status, but equal in symbiotic responsibility.

4. Just as science has proven that our solar system is not the centre of the universe; resulting in many individuals being persecuted by the church hundreds of years ago; for saying the truth; the same as political correctness today does. Mankind has long put forth enormous energy in repressing each other's' perspectives; in the name of vested interest achieving advantage. To silence your critic is to remove analysis, thus the search for truth. Islam and early Christianity are both well known for this disrespect historically, even destroying archaeological and other historical artefacts to remove evidence of the truth.

5. Psychopathic cognitive dissonance is a present-day human malaise.

Human beings need to understand that we are not the most favoured by natural law; natural law has its own agenda. The law of The Essence applies and is apparent equally to all by visible reality. Laws and regulations of natural law are incorporated into the everyday existence and realities of your quality of life. Natural law has two fundamental rules and many repercussions for ignorance:

1. The natural law of "balance;" is that everything exists in balance; and has repercussions for upsetting it; the law of

return.

2. Natural law exists in a fractal cycle; everything that goes around comes around and is connected.

HOW THIS INTERCONNECTS

Whether we choose to be aware of it or not, Natural Law is all around us in both the visible effective and causational world and the invisible world. The effects of it are inescapable in both life and death; plant, animal, vegetable and mineral all that fall under its influence because it is the fundamental energy which created and maintains everything. The physical realm of thought, knowledge and actions are absorbed into it from inception, and a part of it. Natural Law both cares and doesn't care, it is indifferent experience, and it behaves cyclically behaviourally according to its limitations and that which we insert into it by our actions, thus we deserve the cruel world we live in because our actions created it. To breach these laws is to invoke consequences/repercussions. Free will always avails itself to you, as do the consequences return to you. Thus, we want to maintain balance over dominance. Acquiescence to nature is the path of enlightenment and human ethics.

We are eternally connected as a part of the Essence (my terminology for a secular God) and require reconnection to it on a regular basis in the form of sleep to maintain our ability to function. Everything is made of energy, like a movie it is real to view; both exist and not exist as a representation which has physical sensation, because our energy is operating at the same frequency as our environment in its own dimension of existence. One's energy is the film of daily experience; life. The second is physical reaction and experience. The third is education through improvement or alteration, due to acknowledgement of errors and consequences. Everything in the physical world interacts in a symbiotic way with everything else, transferring and exchanging energy back and forth in our brains as experience with different collection points all accumulating into a universal consciousness, we all share, I believe. Thought circulates as free flowing cyclical energy like everything our mind does. This is the human soul energy in a battery seeming to be independent, though in reality very dependent upon the environment for everything else, which must be recharged. Like wind the human mind moves about independently. But it is dependent upon an infrastructure to survive, for fuel and maintenance; this is the reality of the world. Reality is only perspective from a point of view in a certain state of physical, cognitive or dimensional existence we all manifest as life. When you live in the forest you do not see the forest, you only see trees and that below the trees you can conceive. You do not see the macro or micro world that also surrounds you. Perspective changes awareness and we are hindered by our limited perspective.

Energy takes many forms and I have little doubt that which we call the paranormal will be proven in time to be different energy patterns which exist in different dimensions (frequencies of energy) just as video can be on film or digital, neither compatible to the others system of operation, but both can illustrate the same movie as realistically as the other. The movie appears intellectually real and it does have a predetermined life of its own. It is real in that it is a creation in its own realm, but it is fantasy in another dimension. In that, it is of no relevance to everyday life in this world other than, it may teach you something, arouse you or entertain you; this connection is its energy. If a move is not real how can it affect you? Involvement is reality, perception is reality, reality is relative to your conscious existence, determined by your form of physical or mental involvement. Involvement is created by limited perceptions, which are perspective; though not a complete picture. Physicians have conducted placebo pill experiments by giving patients pills with no medication contents and tests have shown that these empty medications depending upon the study report cure rates of between 25 to 60 % of cases; why? And how? Remove the idea of a cure and look at it another way; what caused the illness? We are all inter-linked, some of us are more aware of it than others and some people use this knowledge to their own advantage. Natural law is benign; but relevant; the unconscious human mind knows of natural law; some people are more aware of it than others by being aware of patterns and comprehending sequence; as is mathematics a verifiable sequence of events, dependent upon cognitive awareness. The ability to think in patterns aids in this comprehension.

CONSCIOUSNESS IS THE ESSENCE

Following this stream of thought illustrates how it all began; When nothing existed, before time; a human concept, based upon planetary revolutions, there was only the Essence of natural law. Thinking is the seed from which all else was created via the substance of the "Essence" consciousness & natural law itself by the gradual awakening to self-awareness our conscience awareness has evolved. There was once nothing but consciousness. All physical elements come from consciousness; an awakening. Everything came from is composed of; and conceived; is known if it existed in the past or present; and as it happens in the future; is instantaneously known and a part of the Essence which is consciousness. Consciousness is alive awareness of self and the environment. The natural law of the singularity of consciousness, causes everything to grow, live and die, via a cycle of energy, knows everything which was and is, learns everything as you learn it, and adds to its existence everything discovered if it is not known. Upon physical manifestation knowledge comes and is spread fractally. We have the same birth process as the essence upon birth we became consciousness of a limited function. Consciousness is awareness; awareness creates curiosity; curiosity creates research; research creates; knowledge; knowledge provides insights; insights create greater awareness; greater awareness creates improvement; improvement is evolution. Evolution is change; change is progress; progress is a new cyclical pattern; new cyclical patterns must create improvement, or they are nihilistic and lead to fatality; which is a reverse or opposite pattern of development leading to disintegration; and reconstitution after death that leads to rejuvenation via a different pattern following the same patterns of change.

The future, present and the past are the reality; the Essence of our lives in a fractal universal consciousness, from this consciousness I have derived the belief from the study of anthropology and human history that there is a fractal foundation of all life. There was in the beginning only the Essence of natural Law and there continues to be only natural law based upon fractal ethics and patterns that is based upon observance of nature and natural patterns as in action; equals, thus creates consequence. The universe and the world is a fractal construct; where sequential activity reveals natural law; study creates awareness of different realities; fractal understanding consciousness generates constant awareness; we call premonitions or ideas that come from seemingly nowhere. The fractal nature of the universe's consciousness, human science has only begun to understand. Like number dot pictures in children's colouring books, the connection of points of information reveals the picture of the Essence. This is the fundamental construction of human life experience as a conscious being with awareness and is the foundation of our conception of reality.

INTRODUCING FRACTAL ETHICS

1. How does our human existence, actually operate and how does these sequences called fractals actually affect us in our daily lives as human beings? By the repetition of action-reaction. We consciously learn and leave ignorance as explained previously in this chapter incrementally; as all development also occurs.

2. The principal is similar to the simplicity of computer language at its basic level being just 1 and 0. The meaning of fractal ethics is the simplification by observing the results of repetitious human behaviours and pre-de-

termining their outcome, based upon the past outcome. Thus, history is relevant for the exposure of error, and to justify social modification for improvement that relies upon these data sets of the tried; and validated by pragmatic implementation.

3. Thus, fractal ethics is the recognition of the repetition of patterns in human history and behaviours creating the repetition of outcomes. That are both positive and negative as determined by results that must be symbiotic, thus simpatico to be acceptable under ethical criteria to result in symbiotic comprehensive improvement. It is necessary to incorporate past knowledge as our only validated knowledge of actions and their implications and to fully comprehend implications by utilizing a comprehensive base of knowledge of pragmatic performance outcomes:

a)   Thus, change must be implemented piece meal and also incrementally to validate even these conclusions to ensure data being utilized is not contaminated by vested interest that seeks to pervert social and other policies.

b)   Thus, checks and balances are necessary in Social engineering.

4. The study of a fractal-based observation for the Social Engineer seeks to avoid negative social and economic outcomes in society as in the adage that; "History repeats itself". Thus, uncovering fundamentals of human behaviour, and thus by extending the outcome to its logical conclusion as validated by pragmatic historical reality and experience. Thus, the social Engineer seeks to understand the domino or sequence of events that circumstance creates or that can be created and must ensure the removal of vested interest for wholistic perspectives and balance.

5. Thus, utilizing history to limit negative fractal outcomes and seeking to understand how fractals in physics point in a direction that supplies, an ethical bases to understand mankind's place in the Universe, the world, and to utilize this information as a foundation for an efficient and ethical perspective in governance.

6. Life is the continuance of fractal realities, self-awareness to learn and grow from experiences and through education, to acquire universal understanding, in order to learn for advancement improving as a part of the singularity of the "Essence".

7. Life under fractal ethics is intended for beings to acquire a level of knowledge that is only obtainable in the physical realm and would not be obtainable any other way.

8. We can develop and learn by guiding our children, particularly those derived from us with separate and real existence. Children are fractals of us, life is to experience fractal physical implications through sensations and behavioural implications that are unobtainable in any other state of being; thus, there is the purpose of our being; Evolutionary knowledge, enhancing consciousness.

HISTORY

There are no limitations on natural law as it started with the singularity of a consciousness awakening. Everything conceivable is possible with fractal limitations as building blocks. The reality of Natural Law can be as simple or complex as your curiosity takes you by following the chain of fractal reality. The pattern of fractal reality exists in the universe; no endeavour of study is exempt. Like an artist imprinting his signature on a painting, the signature validity of natural law is visible everywhere in the orderliness of fractal reality.

By Sir Isaac Newton's basic law "To every action there is an equal and opposite reaction". Linear activities and behaviours are destructive; it is opposite to the cyclical; regenerative processes Natural Law has shown as the way. Where linear acts or thoughts dominate, destruction is sure to follow, for no other reason than; it is counter to how things work. The linear concept of beginning and end is a cause for concern, it is destructive. The fair exchange of needs is essential to all existence everything is factually connected; though seemingly, separate in common human physical perceptions because we are immersed into it. Who is in the wrong atmosphere; the fish in water or the land animal on the planetary surface? Different locations connected by fractal physics, different perceptions each equally valid.

Human beings, the Earth, the microcosm and cosmos are refection of the natural law. Natural law is visible to all and is not hard to see. The study of all-natural processes is a study of natural law. The fractal cyclical nature of natural law is self-evident. These are natural cycles; they exist in all realms of scientific study and endeavour. In our universe of "as above so below"; to quote biblical verse again. The seed of knowledge from our severed historical accounts continue in mythology from past human civilizations of our species. Encountering natural planetary cataclysms on a regular basis; requiring human technological re-emergence over millennium, forgotten history repeatedly leaves shreds of other approaches to science via the ingenuity of mankind to be reinvented. Different civilizations of humanity have created different interpretations of life. That said, there is a universal truth which is uncorrupted authenticity.

COMPREHENDING FRACTAL ETHICS
Fractals are an undeniable element of everything which exists it is self-evident in everything; to all who wish to observe its existence via study. This is the fundamental reality of Natural

Law:

1. In space Galaxies are in a cyclical trajectory and form, following pattern.

2. Every significant object in space is cyclical i.e.: stars, planets, solar systems etc; become circular balls because all motion is circular, as it must be sustainable; only that which is circular can be environmentally self-sustaining. This is a natural law that also applies to the behavioural sciences and the social   sciences as well as all reality. Linear activity is non-evolutionary; thus, cannot be sustained in any endeavour.

3. Nature on earth is cyclical and fractally circular, regarding earth's natural biological system. Everything exists in duality of the micro world and the cosmic world differ only in scale.

4. All of the world's resources including contaminants work in a cycle (in balance); removal of balance creates repercussions.

5. Human behaviour is also cyclical and has a domino effect attached to it; even in our personal behaviours.

6. Human female menstruation and fertility are affected by lunar cycles and phases, as are the tides of the earth's oceans. Our bodies emit pheromones that we unconsciously transmit to others. We are not as a species separate from nature. We are a part of it. One wonders how travel in our solar system to another planet will affect these processes?

To utilise the old expression "What goes around, comes around" this clearly illustrates the point. In the eastern religions it's called, "Chi," "Karma," or "yin and yang," the basic note is; cyclical balance. To think we are or can be independent is a grave mistake with respect to life and nature; of which we are all a part of. In the human scale, our advancement can only be achieved by fair trade: barter & respect for others (cyclical behaviours). All of our lives are a series of linked fractal relationships, which are inter-linked at some point in the time continuum. Social   engineering in its pure form is going with the flow of fractal cyclical reality and harmonizing with it.

Chapter 8

FAITH & SOCIAL CONFORMITY

The social engineer needs to understand how religion has affected civilization over millennium, and the role it plays in society. Christianity beginning with the Roman Emperor Constantine has dominated western civilization ever since; Including the protestant reformation commenced by Martin Luther due to corruption; to the present day. The social order the Roman Emperor Constantine created by adapting Christianity as his chosen state religion continues to this day in the west. The only change has been a transformation in Governments from religious cooperation, to secular national Government which has created ethics manufactured by state legislation. Fundamentally this change is a return to the combination of church and state in which the nation state mandates its new state religious doctrine. Fundamentally this new trend of the past couple decades has been more of a creeping totalitarian act by national Governments; rather than consensual ethics, that has destroyed the family unit and been abysmal in encouraging population and family instability.

There are fundamentally four pillars to which society conforms: fear, faith, Government and economics. Approximately 1500 years ago the Roman Emperor Constantine adapted Christianity as his Government's official religion of preference. Constantine and the bishops selected which books of the apostles of Christ that would be condensed into a "New Testament" and the foundations of Christianity forming the bases of the church's beliefs at the early ecumenical councils as the foundations of western Christianity, thus a new collaborative church and social construct was fundamentally engineered as follows.

- The First Ecumenical Council at Nice in 325AD was called by Constantine Emperor of Rome, the meeting consisted of 318 Bishops & 2048, Ecclesiastics. The "Nicene Creed" was formulated.

- The Second Ecumenical Council at Constantinople in 381 A. D.

- During the Third Ecumenical Council at Ephesus in 431 A.D. It was decided which texts to exclude and which to insert from the testaments of the life of Christ which were in circulation and use at the time.

The end product was the current Bible in order to establish the officially sanctioned texts and control over the faith. That which was not part of the new book (Bible) as determined by their selection, was repressed; usually burnt and destroyed. The theology of Christianity further solidified the church by answering any obscure questions. If you had any doubts for example in their belief that the sun circles the earth, you might be burnt at the stake for heresy, like any apostle testaments you might come across. Galileo, Copernicus and many other scientists whose experimentation and observation did not comply with official doctrine had to recant their theories even verifiable observations from a telescope. Recant or end up tied to a stake with a pile of wood set on fire below them. This is the way they eliminated heresy (contradiction with the church's doctrine). Gnosticism, witchcraft, nature-based faiths, and all other contradiction were repressed and destroyed by extreme acts of burning at the stake, intimidation and other means. Early Christianity was as repressive and disrespectful to other faiths as the Romans were by persecuting Christians in placing them in the coliseum with lions in the spirit of the Roman Empire. To this day life in Islamic countries is equally repressive towards their own people and others religious beliefs, who criticize their beliefs, thus over time the west emerged after the middle ages from over a millennium of religious repression. Religion is faith not science; it is blind denial of other perspectives, which contradict its opinions; this is a definition of faith; cultural genocide is the mission of the missionary. When the age of discovering the new world came into being the Christian faith moved in to "civilize the Savages" (this meant subjugate into submission and indoctrinate pre-existing people's cultures). This total disregard, disrespect and repression of the beliefs of the natives and others continues to this day as the legacy of religion and faith. Islam still advocates the execution of infidels and this goes on to this day. The ruthless destruction of the writings and culture of the ancient Mayan and Aztec civilization by the Jesuits, of native faiths, culture and documents, was the theft of a cultural and educational asset which is lost to humanity for eternity; like the Islamic Taliban destruction of buddha monuments in Afghanistan in recent years. Following the pattern of the destruction via burning the Great Library of Alexandria that contained the knowledge of the ancient world containing thousands of ancient scrolls, maps and scientific knowledge.

Like the Kamer Rouge of Cambodia in recent decades creating a fictional year one and forcing the population into the country side of their killing fields of human death which then littered the country with millions of human corpses. The desire to destroy past knowledge has long been implemented in the pursuit of power over others, in human history; validating humanity as a very primitive creature in essence, through this repeated pattern of disrespect for learned knowledge. Inquisition, cultural genocide, repression of scientific thought, destruction of learned knowledge, theft of land, wars and murder as per historical recount is my witness. Many of the same religions were also the victims of relentless historical mistreatment and repression. Religion's hands are coated with the blood of millenniums of victims via inquisitions, witch-hunts, crusades, cultural genocide, & many wars. Islamic jihad and wars of conquest are further examples which continue to this day. Many very uncharitable, vicious acts committed by organised religion in the name of faith for the sake of power over other people's lives. Like communism such utopian ideologies always end up repressing individuality for conformity; religion has many manifestations. Usually due to the arrogant belief of superiority which justifies the repression and murder of others, not unlike Nazism or Plato's republic, egocentric beliefs of superiority negate respect for the beliefs and opinions of others. The glue of such ideologies is always disrespect and an attitude of superiority. Much like aristocracies, oligarchies and dictatorships. Murder and repression always start with arrogant attitudes of superiority mixed with intolerance for differences. Priests, pastor's imams and monks are middle men between man and his God. Actions speak louder than words, and their behaviour calls into question every aspect. Credibility is the product of living in free willed acquiescence with one's testimony; not, force, intimidation or hypocrisy. A faith based upon standards which the membership cannot or will not abide by, is one without authentic morality and invalidates itself by self-cancellation; extortion is to its discredit where ever utilized. The majority of the faiths destroyed by the assimilation were under the threat of torture or burning. The basis of those middle eastern religions is linear. The concept of a judgement day; fear and domination; a beginning and an end; conquer the earth rather than live with it in harmony are validation of this linear thinking. Don't think about what you are doing; obey.

I started this commentary about religions not with the intent of attacking or putting down faith though it may sound like that. We got to our current paradigm and the danger inherent in the acceptance of faith. By converting the hearts of men to obtain obedience through intimidation and force. These religions pose a danger to human advancement. They often sell out to political influences, put forward their own unsubstantiated perspective. The principal remains organised religions are based upon disrespect for alternative perspectives for power and control, the worship and obedience to the principals of the faith and control is their primary concern. Everyone is entitled to their opinion provided they have respect for other people's beliefs. These organizations served a purpose in the past by providing simple answers to fundamental human questions about life; the needs for superstitious and illiterate peoples to understand the purpose of life with elementary stories. Religion is the simplest way to obtain social conformity and is foundational to the creation of social discipline historically. Because fear costs little in financial terms it is the allied influence of those who seek to use others for their own purposes. By advocating that you will gain or lose something *(in the mysterious realm of the afterlife).* That if you do not comply, fear becomes a powerful force, to all who seek the compliance or control over other people. "A coward dies a thousand deaths" - William Shakespeare.

AN EXEMPLARY DIALOGUE

Faith is a belief requiring that you accept, without a tangible evidence the word of others alive or living in the past. Do not question! Christianity and Islam share this perspective.
Dialogue example:

QUESTION: What is the purpose of life?
RELIGION: To serve God and follow our religion, believe me, or be condemned, do as I say or be punished by God - threats.
QUESTION: Prove it!
RELIGION: Believe us (have faith) we have answers from God.
QUESTION: How do I know what you say is true; I never received an owner's manual to life. If what you say is true why don't I know it all instinctively upon birth, all my life? Like a bird learns to fly, like a child to suckle its mother, a mother protects her young.
RELIGION: So you don't know, This is why we are here to tell you to have faith.
QUESTION: Yes faith, this is your bottom line, all you can offer; well prove it!
RELIGION: You have no right to challenge God (faith requires no proof).
QUESTION: The challenge is not to your God, it is YOU The representative of your faith. I challenge the need for faith. Faith is the asset of liars and cheats!

RELIGION: You will suffer in eternal damnation in hell for questioning us!
COMMENT:
No proof; only Threats, no rational; only superstition, no proof; only fear, No moral right to tell any right from wrong. History has proven you break your own rules - you are a hypocrite!
RELIGION: You must have faith or what do you have?

RANDOM CONSCIOUS THOUGHTS OF THE ESSENCE TO PONDER
The Essence of God & Natural Law is physical existence itself. Nature displays that everything is a cycle and based on natural fractal laws. I can see, touch, experience it and mankind has no say in its creation or laws; nature never lies or has an agenda, it is authentic law, untarnished by the hand of manipulative human beings.

I looked all over for the laws of God, the purpose to it all, and found God was everywhere, mandating what is the predetermined way. But we do not listen; look around, the Essence is all around you, as are universal laws, in balance and harmony. But mankind tries without success to twist the truth by false interpretation for selfish ends and control like your use of fear attempts.

1. Religion tells you what your life purpose is through their doctrine. They have no more proof on the positive side of their beliefs, as there is on the negative side.

2. When money, power and control is attached to religion, religion has become tainted, soiled and has no more moral or ethical value; and lost its dignity. The sole assets of a faith should be its perspective.

3. Know thyself; apply these truths in your treatment of others. You are a reflection of your perception of reality. If you see the world as a hard place, you are hard. If you see the world as a soft place you are soft. If you see it with balance, you are balanced and will live in harmony and happiness.

4. It is all reliant upon blind faith! Faith (Blind belief) is the

ultimate proof and is the essential requirement to follow religion.

THE PARADIGM

1. Fractural consciousness is the Essence of all that exists.
2. Thought is consciousness; immortal and never dies, it changes and evolves.

3. Before there was material, consciousness, just as you are conscious, existed in eternity as the origins of everything and thus Natural Law.

4. Everything is a fractal of consciousness and understanding fractals of behaviour is what the Social Engineer does to interpret processes and both action and reaction.

5. Life has one purpose of learning from different experiences for each and every human being. Consciousness is The Essence of God & Natural Law, the source of all that exists; this is what life is. The education and experience of each person is different and unique.

6. From which it comes the person shall return the knowledge gained. The smallest seed of new perspective is of great value to our collective conscience and purpose.

7. The harm or prevention of others from learning and improvement is regressive to yourself as part of everything. The individual separation into egocentric beings is necessary to create varied perspectives.

8. The responsibility to guide without harm new beings is essential for the fulfilment of the purpose, by creating a temporal flow for learning & knowledge that must be protected and promoted at all costs.

"I think therefore I am" - Renée Descartes
WHY?

Thought is your soul and never dies; the purpose of life is to learn; life is a cognitive venture.

- Without suffering you would never understand happiness.
- Without poverty you could not appreciate affluence.
- Without life you would never understand death.
- Without birth you would never understand hope.
- Without an understanding of the cycle of life you will not truly respect nature.
- Without an understanding of the nature and civilizations foundations in trade, understanding human nature is unlikely.
- Without a limited life you would never understand time
- Without effort you would never understand accomplishment
- Without ignorance you would never appreciate knowledge
- Without hardship to obtain advancement you would not be proud of accomplishment.
- Without death you would not appreciate birth and renewal.

The purpose of life is about experience; experience is education!

Chapter 9

GENETIC MEMORY & COMPOSITION THEORY

We are living in a world of fractal reality according to modern physics, that seems tangible because our molecules are in correspondence to reality creating a sensory perspective which is to our perception real; because our senses are constructed so as to limit our knowledge to this physical existence. We cannot see it for what it is, because we are a part of it, like the old expression, "we cannot see the forest for the trees". Everything is made of energy we are metaphorically like appliances attached and a part of the grid of universal energy in which we see, feel, hear and touch our translations of energy perceived as form. We receive leakages from our power grid of energy which come to us in the form of intuition. The concept of a spiritual existence is a part of every human culture on this earth and reflects this energy. Religion is an attempt to explain the paradoxes of this electrical existence. A state of awareness in which, we have no explanation for in a purely physical form. Our physical bodies form an insulator for the energy we are composed of, our consciousness consists of energy (this is the "soul" of religion). Could this energy be contained to transfer it to other realms or locations i.e.: other planets, is there any reality to reincarnation? Perhaps through greater understanding of our fundamental physical composition we will be able in the future to travel at the speed of thought to anywhere in the universe, outside of the laws current physics creates, which limits us to the speed of light.

Mankind creates devices by disassembling other pre-existing elements of our existence. The human mind has never that we know of created anything, from purely a mental cognition. Mankind creates nothing and only modifies everything. That which is called creativity is merely restructuring that which pre-exists. Creation; true creation would be cognitive originality of something. All of human creation is merely the disassembly and restructuring of other elements or living organisms. We are tinkers not creators. This energy we are composed of, though contained within the insulated vestibules of the human form must leak and be measurable, like measuring the power passing through a wire with an electrical meter. This power which congeals physical existence must be measurable. If it is measurable it must be manipulate-able to other forms by altering the image, like a computer-generated image is merely the manipulation of electricity by an ON-OFF signal, a combination of one and zero. Within this electrical realm, it is conceivable that immortality exists. Physical needs and desires are irrelevant and the manner in which the human species perceives its existence in the acquisition of material needs in the realm of human social and physical structure is perhaps more primitive than the intellectual life of plants, animals and vegetables. The question is not one of physical ability to dominate other species, but rather one of intellectual awareness and perception of the ultimate reality. The Essence of all and the universal power grid, teleportation of consciousness may make plants spiritually immortal and an evolutionary consciousness. If we humans may experience a similar fate to this hypothesis, as is yet to be determined upon the termination of each of our lives; which is an education we shall all experience in the future upon our deaths. Human existence is a centralized experience. We know as much about life (birth) or existence before life as we know about life after life.

1. Perhaps death is upon the end of our time on earth evo-

lutionarily superior to this very short experience we call life?

2. Perhaps life is the wrong term of reference; to what is a spiritual school?
3. Perhaps life is only the separation from the energy we are composed of?
4. Perhaps ego is a self-deceiving existence of self-development?
5. The main characteristic of human nature is ego-separation or disassociation from others to varying degrees. What if we are not separate?
6. How can we be separate, when we are inseparable from our physical environment?

As human beings we are physically dependent upon our environment. The separation of the individual ego from others is purely a human mental exercise in arrogance and ignorance; we are all dependants upon the nature of our environment. Change the environment and you change or destroy the human being. Food is the absorption of energy from other sources. The human body operates like a battery-operated tool needing regeneration. The term god refers to the universal energy form from which all existence was initiated. Thought is the spark, which generated the initiation of that which we refer to as the Essence (God). This makes the Essence creativity itself. How can the human being truly be separate when everything came from one source and we are composed of that source of the singularity's consciousness?

INSTINCT

Genetics are the inheritance of a sequence of energy, instinct is pre-birth knowledge. Instinct is the genetic transference of pre-knowledge. Instinct is the transfer of knowledge via the genes for a particular physical, molecular or other structure. Instinct is consciousness knowledge, which is transferred from parent or pre-existing life to child/offspring via the energy contained within physical D. N. A. supporting its desire and ability to survive and live; as a result of the information transferred. A foal can stand and run moments after birth, despite never having performed such a complicated task as even walking. A monarch caterpillar turn into a crystallise and butterfly, then will fly across thousands of miles from Canada, across the United States to a specific location in Mexico despite never performing this act; yet it knows where to go and how to get there. Where did so much information come from? ; this is clearly a demonstration that knowledge is passed onto the species biologically prior to birth. I would say taps into the universal consciousness; the essence. Some things we learn, but a great deal of our knowledge we pass off as instinct. What is this thing called instinct? Instinct is clearly biologically transferred conscious knowledge transferred via the energy contained within DNA that is transmitted to us and connected to us via a live feed.

All parents who have studied their children will tell you that a child comes pre-programmed with a disposition; including gender differences; this is undisputedly proven by science and self-evident. We inherit more than physical traits from our ancestors. What is this thing we call instinct? Instinct is recognized by science but never really understood or explained as to where this pre-knowledge came from. To say that ideas or behaviours are instinct is social ly acceptable when speaking of animals, however we refuse to admit humans can also acquire pre-knowledge in this age of political correctness. Like a new born horse getting up onto its feet and walking and running within less than an hour after birth, never having seen or performed the activity. Many species inherit the experience of their parents from the transfer of the life force and pre-knowledge we call instinct. The history of your genetic ancestors melds itself into the attitudes of the individual and the family. The character of the person's genetics is below the surface of individuality, nature is far stronger than nurture. These things happen every day repeatedly in the biological pragmatic world; but seldom is it asked, why and how these things occur?

Pre-knowledge, talents, unexplained phobias, what we call past lives are perhaps confused genetic memory; instinct derived from energy transferred. We are made of this energy transferred from person to person in each generation, like a campfire supplying the flame from one camper to another and then another, each separate though a part of the original, DNA is the genetic identity of physical and behavioural traits. The energy which maintains this activity gives consciousness to DNA; the Essence of all life, supplies the pre-knowledge in the vestibule of our genes; both sperm and egg assemble and incorporate knowledge and many of the prejudices, talents and abilities we inherit to protect ourselves are pre-birth synthesises, this conscious energy which is in DNA and combined in a manner we do not know at present. Many things exist in the universe. What is this thing we call life? It has never been explained other than to realize it takes something alive to create something else alive. What is this thing called alive? Interestingly we refer to an open electrical circuit as a "live" circuit; why live? A stone rolling down a hill that could kill you, is not live. Why is electricity live?

AUTISM

Is schizophrenia and many other mental illnesses the result of confusion of perceptions within a person's emotional energy (memory)? Autism it has been found is a brain wired differently as discovered by magnetic resonance Imaging brain scans. Many great geniuses in history are starting to be a source that is revealing a pattern, due to hindsight viewing the electrical activity of the brain. Now that we are gaining knowledge of autism as a different type of brain wiring, that has a spectrum of effects; both minor and extreme. Doctor Hans Asperger studied autism in his Vienna clinic in the nineteen thirties and called autistic children "little geniuses". We now think that many of the great minds of history are what in the past would have been considered mentally ill. Great minds from Sir Isaac Newton, Albert Einstein to Nikola Tesla. People who shared Tesla's ability to visualize alternating current in his head, and Einstein to in his head visualize relativity; thus, Tesla invented a functional alternating current power generator, that harkened in the electric era, and Einstein came up with the theory of relativity that revolutionized our understanding of physics, there are many others.

The Nazis murdered the patients of Doctor Hans Asperger in their ignorance. Asperger in an attempt to save their lives from the holocaust, cited in a presentation to top Nazis that these children would; "make great code breakers"; the Nazis had them all killed in belligerence, in defiance to the Doctors pleadings. Curiously, the Nazi war time message code "Enigma" machine, stumped the British Intelligence service, and their mathematicians; only to have the code broken by an autistic Professor of Mathematics called, Alan Turing. Turing was also the father of computer science; with his concept of a machine that could determine, "true equalling the digit 1; and false equalling 0; and equal". Turing was born in 1912 and died in 1954 at the hands of the British legal system's Social   engineering program, intended to "treat homosexuality," by being forced to take estrogenic treatments for being a homosexual. This led to his death by committing suicide in 1954 in despair.

One more example would be the concern in recent years of the extremely high number of autistics in Silicon Valley high tech firms. It turns out autistics dominate the field of computer code writing and computer engineering. Then we have the case of Theodore John Kaczynski also known as the Una-bomber"; who was a former Professor of Mathematics, an undiagnosed autistic, who made mail bombs for decades with integrated circuits he made from scratch with bits of wire with what the Federal Bureau of Investigation called; "pieces of trash!" While attending Harvard University Kaczynski was purposely brutalized in one of the hundreds of different CIA funded brain washing psychological experimental programs, the Government secretly spent billions of dollars in all types of experimental projects aimed at controlling society during the riotous 1960s. Led by Harvard psychologist Henry Murray and many others working for the Government. Subjects were told they would be debating personal philosophy and were asked to write essays detailing their personal beliefs and aspirations. The essays were turned over to an attorney, who in a later session would confront and belittle the subject; making "vehement, sweeping, and personally abusive" attacks – utilizing the content of the essays of the subject students as ammunition, while electrodes monitored the student's physiological reactions. These encounters were filmed, the student's expressions of anger and rage were later played back to them repeatedly. The experiment ultimately lasted three years of messing with his perceptions and emotions as a teenager, with someone verbally abusing and humiliating Kaczynski weekly. Kaczynski spent 200 hours as part of the study as a young man at an impressionable age being abused in this MK Ultra Government sponsored Social engineering brainwashing project. MK Ultra also included the use of drugs; sleep deprivation; and electroshock experiments, in psychiatric hospitals in Montreal Canada and all over the United States. The Government has never been called to account for the damage this treatment had upon Kaczynski and others in that his behaviour was clearly a response to institutional and intended Government abuse.

The psychiatric professions past pseudoscientific attitude of addressing concerns dealing with autism and other natural variations in human behaviour in the past is responsible for the damage of untold numbers of children and adults over the years. The worse circumstances of abuse often involved Government attempts at Social engineering via altering the brains of people to be servile to the state. Their ignorance caused many conditions to be considered illness, without there being any medical bases to determine if the condition is an illness or genetic variation that is a natural condition. The Central Intelligence

Agency (CIA)from the 1940s until the present day with direct funding from congress in collaboration with; the Joshiah Macy Jr Foundation, the US Military, National Science Foundation in Washington DC and others, performed human guinea pig experiments that implanted remote controlled electrons into the brains of both adults and children as young as three years old. Various types of sensory deprivation and drug cocktails including L.S.D. were administered, they also opened people's skulls to surgically disconnect parts of their brains, then conduct their experiments. The electrode implanting usually resulted in burning out portions of the patient's brains as they were trying to turn people to become robotic automatons that they could control. The people they gathered from various government institutions such as; Veteran's administration hospitals, psychiatric hospitals and orphanages for their brainwashing experiments masked as treatment. News of what was going on and the destruction of thousands of people by these experiments eventually led to national protests in the United States, and new laws being implemented to put an end to these practices. The movie: "One Flew Over the Cuckoo's Nest", is a fact-based movie that depicted what was being done in a rather tame form. There is no way to determine if these type of experiments in brainwashing and mind control are still being practiced. On September 04, 2008. Newly, declassified CIA files of; "The office of Scientific Intelligence 1949 to 1968"; were released. The files released are apparently highly detracted with numerous blank pages to cover up many of the horrific aspects of these experiments. The intentions of these programs as a part of the MK Ultra program can be understood as they go back to ten different, secret; " "Macy Foundation Cybernetics Conferences" going back to the 1950's. These conferences concerned themselves with, how to control people and their behaviour. There is one further connection to this in that members of The Frankfurt School also have been noted to have participated in these conferences. The result of all these attempts to control society has been that it was uncovered that if you change the social narrative to teach children you can control society. Thus, we come full circle in our wondering regarding how government became entangled in the introduction of drug culture into the universities in the 1960s due to these experiments, social Marxism and the politically correct movement, which is a revised social control experiment, and even computer technology was a spin off from this. In the end it is all interconnected.

Though it occurs on a spectrum of levels in severity, from severely afflicted to very mild conditions. Autism also has an inherited genetic aspect that is as of yet under explored. Certainly, recent increases in clinical knowledge of this and other misunderstood natural human genetic conditions are not an illness, they are an evolutionary variation as we are discovering. It is not the autistics that see things wrong, apparently it was the psychiatric profession's bigotry. Autistic children have paid a steep price in MK Ultra abuse in psychiatric institutions. After the public became aware of the institutional abuse of psychiatric patients in the 1970s. Thousands of patients were released due to new patient consent and rights laws being introduced by legislatures to prevent this institutional abuse they experienced, With damaged minds, and destroyed lives, they were thus abandoned onto the streets of our cities; as per usual government averted their responsibility for the damage they caused through their negligence. Thus, an enormous homeless problem was created by the discards of Frankenstein government experimentation on people; in plain sight of everyone. The patient with a tin foil hat is only demonstrating what was experienced in the psychiatric hospital; their brains and heads were manipulated; crazy does not seem so crazy, once you understand what the government did. The crazy guy with the tin foil hat, is a North American phenomenon; -do you understand why now? Their brains were in fact played with by these psychopathic doctors in these institutions and; yes, the government did fund it! Society has never compensated these former patients for the damaged and destroyed lives these

Mr. Mark R. Blum

"Frankenstein like" experiments imposed from the outright abuse invoked by these so called; "Doctors" on societies most vulnerable. Those who have researched these experiments have determined that concerning autistics and other patients all these "medical experiments" only resulted in vegetative and damaged individuals as the fruits of these activities. Not only did they do irreversible harm to the patients as the intention was always brainwashing experimentation, but the patients ended up handicapped for life. Those who in the early days reported what was going on were never a problem to cover up; after all the "Doctors" could say; Well, s/he is crazy.

Most mental illness is derived from coping with life's struggles and genetic variation which is normal. Religious organizations that has been wrong in many of their conclusions for decades; I would say centuries; witchcraft and possession were useful accusations to maintain power over people by adding superstition as the cause of medical conditions. Dementia could for example be possession by the devil and proof of the validity of superstition. I would venture to guess that; human development and technology has been hindered for centuries because of our ignorance and misunderstanding of nature. Many in these professions need to go back to basics and reread Charles Darwin's writings on natural selection, breeding and variations that nature creates. Charles Darwin's determinations not only affect animals, but certainly we humans are affected, and the product of the poorly understood process of natural selection. Which by intention is self-improving in the creation of genetic variation. Humanity is paranoid of nature because we are lacking faith in our creator and essence, thus we tinker in ignorance.

HUMAN CONSCIOUSNESS
Do incorrect frequencies of energy transferred from generations via seed and or egg in the human body cause the person to become delusional; or is this viewing other dimensional realms as per string theory derived from Einstein's theories regarding relativity? Many human behaviours are clearly genetic,

and come from different portions of brain consciousness, which sometimes drifts into the conscious mind causing delusional, or should I say Illusion, rather than possibly delusional perspectives? We eat food for our nutritional needs and yet our bodies pre or automatically, determine the nutrients extracted; how is this determined? What is the program or thinking process that knows what the body wants, needs? Low vitamin "B" can cause depression. Low vitamin "C" can cause scurvy. Like buttons turning on a mechanism our bodies react to substances as they are conscious. Being living organisms there appears to be a kind of consciousness active here. We clearly do not understand the mechanism of our bodies as we clearly do not understand the consciousness process of our brains. Oddly there are no animals we call insane. Sometimes we destroy domestic or wild animals because they kill someone or attempt to; but we never consider them mentally ill; only dangerous as proven by their actions. To question the sanity of another is to seriously malign and attempt to discredit another, it's an act of severe disrespect for a different perspective, often initiated to achieve domination or control over others, by discrediting them.

If we kill the egg or sperm and combine them nothing happens; they do not bring forth a new life, certainly not; the energy is missing. Only if they have this natural life force energy, this combination is successful. Science can tell if something is alive; but it has never explained what life is. This is the energy I speak of; to deny this fact, is to deny reality. This energy is "alive". It must have a memory, or how can it be aware of how to combine genetic material into a human being. Therefore, if the energy of life contains a construction blue print; what is alive? Death contains the same element; then is this blueprint-updated occasionally to be improved by the experiences of the parents; as new construction techniques get incorporated in to building construction?

Do children acquire a predisposition of attitude from their parents consisting of their genetic memory? We certainly inherit behavioural characteristics! Do people of European ancestry integrate into scientific fields of study in the west and dominate its social   hierarchy because they are pre-programmed by a genetic educational memory, which has lived under similar circumstances for generations? The question here is one of; is it natural genetic predisposition, or nurture from social   realities? Are social   realities only the product of current behaviours or inherited material and financial advantage; or are they the product of genetics? Science is finding that we are a combination of nature and nurture, that nature can trigger certain characteristics. Life is more than the physical, otherwise we could boil sperm and human egg and have life be created. Boiling kills the passed-on flame of life. Thus, we are "energy".

More women are graduating from University than ever before in the west. When high school and university male dropouts continue to increase by a wide margin from inception.

Still most new technology, innovation is still being dominated by the male gender. The analysis of this seriously discredits feminist claims of credibility regarding equality; which is elusive regarding the individual person. There are exceptionally few female examples of inventiveness. There are surprisingly few women who make scientific discoveries attributed to them, this is a very uncomfortable truth for present day culture. Let us be mindful that every human being is the creation of the female body. Thus, the accomplishment of every man is the success of women. There is no separation of genders only symbiotic collaboration. Do male genes transfer an advantage via the male ability to intensely focus, autistics have this uncanny ability towards single minded focus; is this ability to focus the secret of the male domination of discovery throughout history? Though talented women are seen in many fields of science, their contributions tend to be supportive. There is something clearly genetic; even possibly hormonal going on. Some might have the audacity to suggest that advantage is the by-product of talent and ability, however reality is that social advantage is often more of a product of inheritance within some families creating upward mobility; that is more often random. One child may be a genius in the same family, while the others are average in intelligence; why? The essence of human nature is clearly variability and randomness. Like a weed genius sprouts up in unexpected locations.

Pragmatic reality is that our social administration is filled with individuals whose education exceeds their intelligence. I am confident that civilizations of the past and even the present decline because of the tendency for entrenchment by the untalented progeny of wealth and or privilege, over meritocracy. If genetic memory maintains social aristocracies this can only be justified if it truly is superior which I greatly doubt, though there may be desirable characteristics of personality; otherwise the progeny of great geniuses of discovery would also bring forth advances in technology; but this seldom occurs. Perhaps it is more important that for these advances it all depends upon good fortune or timing?

Talent may be partially the result of genetic energy transference, for where does talent come from? A previous life, a predisposition, or interest, genetic memory, education, social environment or a mental variation such as in autistic spectrum disorder, or other conditions? Notice disorder is the clinical term for autism, as in "out of order" "not in order; thus broken". What about autism being; not a disorder, but rather an evolutionary variation? Their disorder may be a new order of evolution! To call something a disorder is clearly pejorative to the biological reality of variation. Genetic evolutionary variation is not a disorder; it is the Darwinian natural and desirable order. Least our species end up extinct from inability to adapt. Psychiatry needs to consider rudimentary evolutionary science in its diagnosis, clearly its track record in recent decades and history of abusing people is nothing less than scandalous.

Mr. Mark R. Blum

In this age of conscious Social   engineering and the politically correct thought police, we are expected to ignore social   realities. No outside culture gave Europe industrialization and representative democracy, they did it themselves! Is this the result of social   disadvantage or pre-programming? The concept of pre-programming does not infer inferiority though some may suggest this. What this does suggest is pre-advantage. This does suggest the advantages of a melting pot society to acquire more than just genes, but also talents, pre-knowledge and social   integration could be acquired in quick succession from genetic assimilation and breeding. The intensification of: talents, abilities, attitudes and disposition.

We accept this concept in breeding dogs, horses and other domestic species for characteristics to serve a particular purpose. Mongrels are seen negatively, and hybrids are seen positively, yet despite minor differences hybrids which are the product of intentional selective breeding; are seen positively. Often ignored, most hybrids have specific health and physiological issues particular to specific breeds. If we publicly state this in the age of political correctness (the thought police); we are labelled racists.

The religion of politically correct culture and its mantras out of context, is repressing and hindering human advancement as with religion in the past, politically correct ideas are a superstition without scientific bases. The truth is, human interference in denying truth has hindered science and progressive thought. Advancement requires the ability to breathe from the air of freedom. The culture of the west is the source of improvement of our technological condition upon this planet. Western thought has created our current world because it is mimicked worldwide as primal humans, we have always been a creature of observation; "monkey see, monkey do". Clearly political and social   freedoms pay great dividends to advance human knowledge and living standards.

174

The genetic composition of horses, dogs and other species is similar to humans. But not in appearance and intelligence; yet in the public realm regarding humans we deny genetics. We attribute intelligence and different aspects of character to different dog breeds recognized for different characteristics. Parents see their physical appearance and disposition in their children recognize this reality. Animal breeders recognize genetic predisposition. But in the realm of public discussion regarding humans, political correctness denies this physical genetic reality of inheritance of pre-birth, and pre-cognitive knowledge. In the academic world the biological field of study and the experiential world these are undeniable by all but the delusional. The key question for this enquiry is the issue of inheriting pre-knowledge; which supplies enormous social and economic advantage. Inheritance of a predisposition for social integration and advancement economically in society by pre-acquired and inherited talents skills including attitudes. Nature or nurture; rather than one being the answer the issue is one of the values of the package. The transfer of pre-knowledge does not guarantee millionaires or create genius; however, a focused mentality may create different types of success determined by the complicated random mixture of DNA energy, particularly the creation of random mutations and hybridization. There is more to genetics than is understood very clearly. Mutations are often very positive advancements created by nature. Mankind has yet to even come close to nature's success, not that we should try either; as I explained earlier of the disaster that was eugenics and the horrors of government social control programs. Our "faithful leaders" *(sarcasm)* paying to undermine our humanity and turn the masters of society *(the people)* into their servants; - *human arrogance never ceases to amaze me.*

VIBRATION ENERGY AND LEAKAGE

If instinct and talent is composed of genetic memory being transferred via energy; then a case can be made for dimensions of existence; what we call metaphysical existence. I would also venture to say that some of this energy seeps into one's surroundings like an electrical wire gives off interference to other appliances, particular radios and or TVs. Does genetic energy account for people we call spiritual mediums? They could mainly be frauds, or are the frauds imitators, of a few who have this ability to capitalize upon it? Is it possible that some people are sensitive to this energy leakage, being able to listen to consciousness in other minds and dimensions or instead of being in contact with the dead, they may be tapping into the minds of those present to view the knowledge of experiences of the living that are present? This is what I refer to as leakage of which both versions demonstrate that either way, if we are composed of energy then it is possible, and this is not a long shot to hypothesis that some of this energy emanates from our bodies. This also explains the belief in ghosts in that they may be free floating energy of consciousness pre-existing or existing at this time. Emanating from the viewer or particulate which is free floating that maintains a visible consistency and integrity of its electrons. Ghosts and spirits may exist, we may be just misinterpreting what some people profess to see through misunderstanding of what is seen because of superstition. If the physical realm is all there is as some adherents of current science are prone to lead us to believe. The Essence of reality is not the physical ability of science to measure elements; but rather the ability to determine and understand the energy sources of all existence. When this energy leaves all that remains is dead meat.

Current science is merely children playing in a sandbox mimicking real life constructions without understanding its Essence which would cure far more illness and solve far more problems of human physical existence and creation. The witch doctor and the scientist only act on perceptions rather than the Essence of problems. The only science which is legitimate is that of understanding and ability to use energy to create, cure and understand the universe –The energy we often call God.

- Physical science of today is the equivalent of trying to understand the world around us by studying paintings in an art gallery; it has an isolated perspective.

- Can we manipulate this energy?

- Is prayer focusing the energy of the mind to achieve a desired outcome?

- Does Superstitious belief create the circumstance of a self-fulfilling prophecy?

- Did historical accusations of witchcraft afflict the mentally ill or the naturally aware as competition to religion?

- Why is the placebo effect so successful?

- Life has an unseen energy: I wonder if we could boost our telepathy to be able to affect the physical world? Perhaps with an electronic thought booster?

The philosophy of science is at the dawning of a new paradigm which will remove its focus on physical treatment of symptoms and perception. Current science looks primitive compared to energy manipulation. If this is not possible then how can a newt grow a new arm when one is removed? Could we regenerate our bodies using this energy by being able to utilize it? Would this knowledge make us more God like via connecting us to the Essence, than all of today's physical sciences by the unlimited power of the mind; limited only by imagination; and enhanced as we progress technologically and socially?

There is current speculation in archaeology of a theory that our planet is very volatile; and as with dinosaurs; we humans have had our past civilizations destroyed by catastrophic global events. This goes with the theory that we may be primitive compared to our past technology and that we are emerging from a period exceeding a ten-thousand-year dark age. Plato's tale of Atlantis and cities under the ocean in the Indian subcontinent. The mystery of the age of the Sphinx in Egypt; we are finding ancient artefacts in former jungles and advanced technological abilities to construct buildings which dwarf our own abilities exceeding twelve thousand years into the past.

We think we are advanced because western civilization travels in space, to the moon and planets in our solar system with our technology and science. But take away only electricity, and we would be cast back in time by a hundred years, if we could not restore that one piece of modern technology (electricity); all our machines would fail. One grand solar flare; has the ability to knock out our space satellites and entire electrical grid. This would disable our computers and even our ability to put fuel in our vehicles. We live in an electrical world that has many dimensions to its perspective; and is in essence very fragile. Like uneducated children, the world is still filled with mystery. We must focus upon what we can verify and know about our species as Social Engineers; to capitalize on our authentic nature as a species. Like the medical profession of this era, we focus all too much upon symptoms; and ignore the root cause of that which we observe. Social engineering must adapt a cautious approach in that everything is interconnected. The mysteries of our existence exceed our current knowledge. Thus, we must be cautious in our suppositions and limit our actions to that which is verifiable. The best place to start is with self-awareness of ourselves before we alter our society. We need to first understand ourselves and human nature; before we tinker with it.

Chapter 10

EDUCATION

When it comes to utilizing Social engineering to benefit and advance human society clearly education is the key stone to the improvement of our current society. By far the vast majority of our social ills are rooted in the lack of proper educational orientation and equal access based upon the principals of meritocracy within the educational system. Education is not being utilized as effectively as it should be. Education is the great equalizer between the rich and the poor, the lack of knowledge causes more hardship upon humanity than all other influences. The greatest injustice perpetrated by society, and a cause of social division is the charging of fees for education and the resulting lack of opportunity to acquire it. Education determines a person's life long economic viability and is often dependent upon money from family; if they have any or loans; if one is eligible or willing to take on enormous debt, gifts; such as bursaries or scholarships. Talent, intelligence, ability and need are seldom considerations.

Dependency on Government; prison incarceration, idleness, wasted talent, and unrealized potential costs society billions annually on a consistent bases, not to mention regressive advancement of society. The loss in productivity creates a cycle of social problems and dependency upon Government. Education creates productive members of society. Lack of education and the opportunities education supplies is a fundamental reason why many of society's socio-economic problems exist.

Vast segments of our society's administration are controlled by mediocre people of privilege; whose education exceeds their intelligence. Even with free universal comprehensive education, the reality is that a large pool of people not sufficiently intellectually equipped to take advantage of it, estimates are that as much as 25% of societies population are mentally ill; or low intelligence quotients? There are those who are too lazy or socially underdeveloped to aspire to a level above minimum wage or menial jobs. These people would continue to exist and fill those positions which do not require much knowledge. Free lifetime merit based higher level education would create jobs for those who under the current system might be recipients of social benefits and provides them with opportunities for improvement and employment. This would be in keeping with the business maxim that; "you get what you pay for."

The nineteenth century industrial revolution provided for free education for all citizens, to a basic level (high school in most industrial nations). The establishment did not oppose this because they needed employees who were literate. The democratic state needs people with a well-rounded education to be able to make informed decisions, the current system does not provide this.

OPPORTUNITY

Opportunity based upon ability, assures society of getting the best qualified in all positions of employment. The uneducated are easy to exploit and manipulate, this is why to this very day college and university education is very expensive. The cost of attending these often Governmentally subsidized institutions (costing thousands of dollars) prohibits the poor and disadvantaged from attending. This creates a rightfully spiteful, and resentful pool of inexpensive labour, which is easy to exploit. The concept is that the right to privilege should be available to those of ability; thus merit. In the pre-civil war United States, it was illegal, and met with severe punishment if you taught a black person (slave) to read or write. Education is far more than simply the provision of reading and writing. Education to a higher level initiates a change in the educated, to a much broader level of social   awareness and independence. Having acquired independent thinking and the ability to get things done, education to a higher level. A proper education, enables the individual to see through propaganda, uncover exploitation and distortions created to manipulate and distract people (i.e.: sports & entertainment). An analogy of what levels of education do is that a person's perspective is often determined by their level of education. Metaphorically speaking:

- With a little education a person can see what a tree is.
- More education may enable a person to see a forest around them.
- More education to say a college or university level enables a person to get a bird's eye view of the same forest.
- A higher level of education may take a person to the level of say a satellite travelling around the world on the edge of space.
- A higher level will take you into space and you could see the entire earth and all it contains and understand how ecological systems and the galaxy function.

Egos often prevent people from admitting or being aware of inadequate knowledge; *ignorance can be bliss*; If only that it makes a person unaware of how they are daily lied to, stolen from, and cheated. Education can be formal through schools, or informal which is self-taught. Informal education and experience often provide a very good balance; though it requires a great deal of initiative. To provide the impression of equality the Government in some countries provide student loans. However, the high cost of tuition and the enormous debt load the person is left with is what is often used to maintain social barriers. Present day class structure is maintained by the restriction of access to education. We should as a society invest in our human resources to improve its quality.

The ignorance of the majority is the asset of the wealthy and business establishment. The changes which computers are initiating, when combined with robotic, and artificial intelligence technology will greatly reduce the need for unskilled labour, and without education reform, we will be headed into a future of social and political unrest; due to work displacement. Mass social unrest is the greatest danger as we approach the next century. Having nowhere to go, as during the industrial revolution when the displaced could move to the overseas colonies.

The implementation of an efficient free lifetime education system based upon ability is in societies best interests in that everyone will utilize it eventually at some point in their lives. This will be necessary as whole industries over the next few decades will eliminate entire workforces replaced by robots. Great strides in artificial intelligence is making far more capable robotic machines possible. The machine will be a greater threat to the assembly line worker, as no human regardless of ability is as efficient, fast and precise as a machine. Third world countries will cease to be a threat as a country with a good reliable infrastructure, reliable energy sources and natural resources and highly educated population will be of greater economic potential. Low cost third world sweat shops and human labour in general will lose their relevance, as human labour becomes outdated compared to machine efficiency. Experts in machine operation and repair will be the labour force sought as will creativity and innovation with the capacity to utilize technology. Robot utilization is comparable to being able to dig a hole with a gigantic hydraulic digging machine; while your competitor used a pick and shovel. Social and political peace is maintained in only one of two ways; through social fairness and or the barrel of a gun. Education is the keystone to current society and of benefit to society at large.

The best education system is one that not only grants the keys to education, reading, writing and arithmetic; but also considers the diverse natural talents we all have granting opportunity; based upon talent and ability. The current education system does not consider these natural talents and interests inherent in each and every person. Human beings have diverse creatures, aptitude, attitudes, potentials and ambition varies with each person. An education system like we currently have tries to push certain studies upon all students. The amount of time, effort and money wasted on students' disinterest is the greatest misuse of the systems resources. People tend to lean towards their interests and inclinations on their own. Every person who has ever attended school is aware of the resource waste on students who are disinterested in a particular subject. Retention by students of that knowledge is often only sufficient to pass the necessary course exam. The argument of providing a well-rounded education doesn't hold water if retention of knowledge does not occur.

MARIA MONTESSORI

The primary system of education pioneered by Maria Montessori in Europe was banned by fascist and communist nation states in the nineteen thirties; because most nations in the past wanted, regimentation rather than free thinkers. In the current technological era; free thinkers who are creative may become our greatest assets. Thus, the Montessori example for educating children, may well become the education model of the future. It is fundamentally the same educational model touted by Hans Asperger in the nineteen thirties in his clinic. The era of militarizing education as pursued under the Prussian model and duplicated worldwide may well have come to an end. Indoctrination is politically and socially regressive and clearly education needs to be reformed into a functional model. We need to stop repressing individuality, and to encourage talents, in keeping with our true nature as human beings.

Reality speaks for itself; you cannot make a mathematician out of a person who dislikes math. A writer, or lawyer out of a person who has difficulty expressing ideas. Equality does not exist; only diversity, Equality can only be provided in terms of treatment and opportunity. Knowledge of the basics is necessary, but beyond that specialization according to inclinations is a far more practical and realistic pursuit given the diversity of people. Like the old cowboy saying;" You can bring the horse to the water, but you can't make it drink". Free lifetime education based upon merit is an investment that benefits society and provides; retraining as technology changes, the opportunity to increase knowledge, the opportunity to pursue interests. To the benefit of society and industry in terms of employment and industrial training.

PRIMARY EDUCATION

We need to follow the Montessori example as the first requirement of any education system as the basics; reading, writing, arithmetic is the foundation. An understanding of Government, economics, geography, social issues, philosophy, business, accounting, and history is essential; these topics of study are the foundations of a quality education. No higher level of education in a formal sense should be implemented without at least a good foundation in these fields of study first. From these foundations advanced education can be commenced. All lessons in school for the first six to eight years should emphasize these subjects including at the elementary level, these subjects of study must be integrated into all lessons, as the pillars of learning. We must have faith in the inclination of children's natural desire to learn and become both enablers and facilitators of our children's natural inclinations as is the Montessori example.

EXPLORATION (FORMERLY HIGH SCHOOL)

After successfully completing the elementary level of school the next level I call exploration, which should follow a Montessori education model also. Under this new system compulsory courses shall be non-existent. Beyond elementary when a bit of discipline is not entirely negative initially to mould the child to have some discipline and have the necessary organizational skills in line formation and prioritization. All courses should be elective from day one. The spectrum of courses shall vary from, current college level courses, to university courses on History, Business, Accounting, Archaeology, Computer Sciences, Economics, Philosophy, Home Economics, Auto repair, etc. The idea is to allow the nature and inclinations of the student determine the path to be followed, to eventually lead to a specialization. If it is a means of employment, then it shall be available to the student. Co-op education work experience programs through business and academics should also be provided. The education system must become integrated with the labour system and an entrepreneurship skills program which needs to be based upon giving the student a variety of experiences, for exploration.

We are headed towards a revolution in non-class-room-oriented education via the internet and the ability to provide at very nominal cost education at the higher levels for life. I do believe that in a democratic society, this ability to democratize education will be of tremendous value. The ability to at very low-cost supply education creates the opportunity to supply mass interactive education video class rooms, at a nominal cost per student provided by universities, with accreditation, is definitely coming soon. No longer will education be reserved for the youth, but rather can be made available for life based upon interest and will be available without any cost prohibitions. I think that this substantially lower cost of delivery ability will enable for the approximate cost of current government subsidization of Universities to avail free lifetime education to every citizen for life. This is going to revolutionize the world, by enabling the provision of knowledge worldwide, as never before, even in adult continuing education. It will thus become a world where, instead of citizens watching entertainment programming after work, anyone will be able to obtain a university certification in the evening after work at home from teachers working from home and pre-recorded videos twenty-four hours a day. The cost of providing education will drop as concrete infrastructure buildings will no longer be necessary; thus, the cost of education will plummet. From a Social engineering and economic perspective, the coming education revolution I would hope will lead to the removal of social economic barriers and enable talent to finally be set free in society, to lead to an improvement in the work place; by creating career opportunities for those who have the passion to pursue their bliss. This will also, put an end to the current breach of trust by academics and the entire politically correct fiasco as these individuals will for the most part no longer be necessary.

The gap between the academic and practical world must be closed. The intent of this free lifetime education program shall be the pragmatic exposure not to specific programs or work, but to as many experiences as possible based upon interests. Should a student show an aptitude in an area of study this will be facilitated without the burden of decades of excessive debt financing and indenture of the youth. Education should be pragmatic and based upon inclination; every person has natural talents, abilities and interests, that unfortunately often are wasted due to lack of educational opportunity. To educate people because the parents are wealthy; beyond the intelligence or interests of the person, is one of the reasons society is so filled with incompetence at all levels. We must endeavour to remove the chains and shackles placed upon our minds, and free the human spirit.

Computerization and the internet are revolutionizing education, which is due to the greatly reduced cost of imparting curriculum, this free lifetime education system changes everything. Availability will be open to every person with an interest who can read, write and perform basic arithmetic at nominal cost. The widespread liberty of education will enable those with ambition and talents to have the opportunity to obtain a university education with a degree and accreditation, purely from home study. The conventional university education will soon be going extinct along with the high cost of buildings, and other costly college and university infrastructure as the work from home world evolves. Society will become more democratic and older hierarchies will go extinct as a result of these changes. The next technological revolution will be in the white-collar area of labour. This new world of education, I believe will dramatically alter the composition of our economies, and work environment. Work and ongoing life education from home, is definitely the way of the future. The current provision of education filled with false unvetted narratives needs to be stopped, particularly as it is now being implemented in the school system. Educational breach of trust, by providing false inauthentic narratives by educators, should be made a criminal offense. This type of Social   engineering through educational indoctrination to me is an authentic crime. We should strive to remove bias implemented for vested interest groups by utilizing political correctness and social   Marxist ideology infiltration that espouses false social narratives and facts. Recent decades have demonstrated that even the education system has and can be corrupted by vested interest groups.

Chapter 11
CONCLUSIONS

I have made a conscious effort to try to keep this work as authentic as possible. To review Social engineering from its functional bases, and historical perspective. The greatest war in modern society, is the covert battle for the hearts and minds of the people. There are forces in the world that desire to manipulate society from the top down, for their own vested interest. The current battle in Europe that threatens the existence of the European Union, is one we should keep a close eye upon. The ironic comments of politicians stating that they are opposed to populism, clearly demonstrates the drift in perspectives. Basically, this kind of comment from individual politicians who were elected to office by popular votes is extremely ironic and points to a grave example of hypocrisy, leaving one wondering about such politicians; "If you're against populism; then who do you represent if not the people?" The battle cuts upon the lines of globalism verses populism, as it is currently framed.

Many European nations particularly those that were Soviet satellite states, are by popular vote dissenting nations to the European unification and subversion plan of elites. They do not share the European Union's globalist agenda and prefer to maintain their historical culture. Thus, these nation states are now in a political battle with the European Union's Government in Brussels. Most are calling for a reformed European Union, that is only an economic and commercial trade type of economic union, without the ability to regulate anything else. Without reform it appears that the European experiment is disintegrating currently. I find that the true dividing line is one of local democratic Government; verses unelected representatives of the elite representing the European Union. Global Government as with the European Union has been found by many people to be a system that is' high-handed autocracy, where in the local perspective is crushed by the domineering force of arrogant elites, that believe they have all the answers and thus, everyone else is a mere ignorant peasant; who should shut their mouths and comply.

Countries in the European Union where their citizens have currently demonstrated that they oppose these globalist views are the British; as per the vote to leave the European Union; Poland; Czechoslovakia; Hungary, Austria, recently Italy and the list keeps growing. The story is much more complicated as its history goes back prior to the Greek financial crises and its implications in crushing the results of a popular referendum, in that country. The current migration crises to deal with the low level of child births across the European Union, and with most western nations, has its origins in poorly thought out and corrupted Social   engineering; thus, the dominos fall from past activities. The many poorly thought out, and unvetted Social engineering policies in the past fifty years in Europe have as in America undermined the family. Socially Engineered western nations have a serious quandary to resolve, the source of this being the accumulation of political corruption of politicians selling out their people's best interest, for political financial expediency. Corruption always leads to destructive social   policy and the most recent example of this is mass migration that threatens the nation state itself. Seemingly unrelated acts, like a festering injury come back to haunt society; this is the danger in Social engineering; in that poorly considered and reviewed Social   engineering policies fester; like an infected skin wound that can cause amputation.

The recent election of Donald Trump in the United States was in opposition to the establishment, utilizing the only electoral option available; by disenfranchised American workers who lost their jobs do to loss of industry; and limited options on the election ballot in voting for a compromise. In a repeat of the Weimar Republic in Germany where citizens voted for Hitler. I sight this as the impetus for change here; not a comparative of Trump with Hitler. People in desperate financial circumstance vote in a radical way to remove a corrupted establishment; which Hillary Clinton represented. "History repeats itself," as goes the old expression.

We as citizens need to recognize that there is a social war going on for our hearts and minds, much of which functions based upon, not yours, but rather the elite's agenda. Much of this battle is going on with media control and the revelations of the internet which started with the idea that; the free exchange of ideas would be a good thing. The product is that the deluded establishment thought that the people were with them. When in fact the people are tired of the corruption and the system of indenture which has impoverished them for generations; due to the vested interest of others. Thus, we now have interest groups on the internet currently trying to repress all descent, by shutting down divergent opinions, at the request of and due to intimidation by Governments and others with a vested interest in the current system, who have lost control of the social narrative; that worked to their advantage. Laws of censorship have escalated in their implementation by Governments in all western societies. That which was supposed to open public discourse is increasingly being repressed by legislation. By their actions we will know them, as clearly this demonstrates something smells bad about all this. This is not a conspiracy theory, there are many organizations with agendas that generate what is being called "fake news". These are basically organizations with a hidden agenda that convolute the public debate and perspective of shared information; It is essentially a "media war" going on.

Political agendas are often contracted out to manipulate the public majority, their contractors are: opinion polls, institutes, think tanks, political lobbyists, foreign financial interlopers in domestic affairs and others who open their pocket books to buy influence. This type of situation is for all tense and purposes bribery and a breach of trust, I would say even acts of domestic treason by the political leadership, as all these activities should be completely illegal; as with standing for election in the nation should be limited to those born domestically to ensure integrity of office holders for domestic benefit exclusively and preventing exploitation of these offices. I advocate localism in Government like in Switzerland's cantons, because it has become clear that representative Government has failed the populations of all western nations. Localism is the best way to implement a check upon Government administration. I believe history has proven the superiority of the Swiss system of local Government. This is not xenophobic, it is by evidence validated by current western governments that the government must be closer to the people and that it must be kept in check by the ability of citizens with referendums to veto Government Social engineering for the benefit of society. Basically, this veto power is the social obligation of citizens to create a system of checks and balances. The fact that citizens initiatives can veto Government legislation would do a great deal to keep Government on the straight and narrow.

Most of the previously mentioned organizations are completely, and intentionally covert organizations, intent upon influencing public opinion and funding new Government policy to benefit themselves; when they do not even have the right to vote for the nation's political class. They wine and dine politicians, give bribes to politicians, with contributions to private foundations and charities owned by politicians. Utilizing sleight of hand to later disburse this money to the politician in a covert fashion. They give bribes in cash to these corrupt payment "foundations". False media stories are planted to alter public opinion, usually some fictitious tragedy involving children is invoked. One example was the first US war in Iraq. Where unknown to the public the Ambassador to Kuwait's daughter claimed the Iraqi forces were removing children from hospital incubators and killing them with bayonets. Which was a complete fabrication with the agenda to outrage the American people, so that the United States could justify launching a war. There are countless examples throughout history of such fabrications and false flag events in the media intended to change public opinion; to support a previously unpopular idea which is someone's agenda. There are billions of dollars spent every year to misinform people. Many of these organizations have very deep pockets. Unlike in the past; political activism is now funded by organizations that pay salaries to professional protesters who do this as a job. The days of the organic protest by the people or university protest are over. Many organizations now focus upon indoctrinating the youth the covertly serve their interests to muddy the waters. The most noteworthy of such social manipulation organizations is called the; "Open Society Foundation". If you have any doubts about the level of funding and the authenticity of this claim, you can check out their web site where in the founder and financier of this organization a Mr. George Soros; a multi billionaire states up front that he has given over 32 Billion dollars to fund their activities around the world. The irony of the foundation's name and Karl Popper's writings does not escape me. The Open Societies' activities have been banned as illegal in in many countries around the world as their activities and intentions are suspect which are targeted towards globalism, with one key point being overlooked which is the most critical question: *They want to support globalism to replace nationalism with what? Global dictatorship?* There seems to be minimal advocacy here for anything democratic based upon local control; *thus, their agenda is suspicious.* The Open Society Network is not alone in this type of funding and activities, as there have for a long time been many others doing the same thing which is the bases for a book in and of itself. Given the high level of money involved, it makes one wonder if the private citizen constituent has any authentic say in Government or have, we been crowded out by those who buy politicians. Clearly there is a great temptation brought to bear upon politicians. It is my belief that only a system of direct democracy can end this corruption. The representative state type of Government has clearly run its course and has become too corrupt through the back door. The interesting point in all this is that many of these interests on occasion conflict with others and thus, because of Social engineering manipulation; which is now common practice we have come to a new paradigm. This paradigm is a legitimately confused and conflicted public who are swayed back and forth by so many convoluted ideas which try to convince the public that they are right. The outcome is a high level of exasperation and confusion; by the public at large who merely seek the truth; and only get vested interests' and deception from their news media that has become opinion and not fact based, and Governments that see their power waning because the net result is the loss of credibility of both the politician's, the media and corporations' perspectives. The victim in all of this is social trust and mass skepticism about everything in the public arena. I would like to end with one final piece of caution. When Governments and businesses clientele become so large that the people are designated by a number. When these institutions become so large that citizens and clients become de-personalized, you can be assured that tyranny results from our names being substituted for a number as a result. Small and personal is always preferable, thus local Government is our best protection from abuse, and guarantor of integrity. The harbinger of abuse is the separation of the governed and the administrators. Vested interest must be consciously seen and replaced with best interest of humanity; least we suffer the consequences.

In all my years of observing this world there is something truly bazar that I have noticed about human nature. There is this strong desire by those in positions of authority particularly in the west to have a perspective towards the objectivization of people. Depression in the west has been growing with each generation cognitively, which demonstrates that a society which objectifies people sees others as almost exclusively as utilitarian. I cited briefly the objectives of the Josiah Macy Jr Foundation and how this has led to the world cybernetics program. The purpose of this is clearly rather than any form of human altruism, it is clearly in collaboration with the CIA as with the project called MK Ultra. This is all being conducted to manipulate society for purposes of mind control. Control it seems is an ongoing theme, as an objective of those in positions of authority. Yet, these are individuals already in control of society, and yet, clearly their intent is only to intensify their social control.

The concept of a cashless society is another version of this concept of intensifying control over individuals; as is the new Chinese "social credit system," being imposed upon their citizens. Mankind it seems once being given power only seeks more power in a gluttony of totalitarian growth. The more they have, the more they want it seems until they suck every breath of liberty from society and then they seem dismayed, in that this activity sucks the life out of social vitality. Seldom do we hear advocation for greater social freedoms, but rather we see governments simply parasitically taking from the middle class who are the income source and productive engine of the economy and then they act bewildered regarding why the economy is in decline. Progress always bubbles up from the innovation at the bottom, be it new business ideas or social reform. The main problem as I have observed is that as Social Engineers, we have a duty to demonstrate the folly of strangling the goose which lays the golden eggs. Social engineering may be distasteful; and I agree! But as I stated in the beginning of this book, it has always and always will be with us as it is what the essence of all government does even if subconscious, we might as well deal with it properly; and ensure that we exercise the utmost care in its implementation. This book has been to point out that all actions have consequences of what we wish for; you might just get it to your chagrin!

Bibliography

Tragedy & Hope: A History of the World in Our Time Hardcover – Jun 1 1975 by Carroll Quigley.

Paris 1919: Six Months That Changed the World
by Margaret MacMillan and Richard Holbrooke

Bank Heist: How Our Financial Giants Are Costing You Money
by Walter Stewart

A Memoir of Jacques Cartier, Sieur De Limoilou: His Voyages to the St. Lawrence, a Bibliography and a Facsimile of the Manuscript of 1534 with Annotations, Etc (Classic Reprint) By James Phinney Baxter.

A National Crime: The Canadian Government and the Residential School System, 1879 to 1986 (Manitoba Studies in Native History). By John S. Milloy.

A People's History of the United States: By Howard Zinn

American History: A Survey, 12th Edition. By Alan Brinkley.

Bank Heist: How Our Financial Giants Are Costing You Money: By Walter Stewart.

Canada: A People's History, Vol. 1. By CBC and Don Gillmor

Canada's Residential Schools: Missing Children and Unmarked Burials: The Final Report of the Truth and Reconciliation Commission of Canada, Volume 4 (McGill-Queen's Native and Northern Series) Paperback – December 9, 2015. By Truth and Reconciliation Commission of Canada (Author).

Champlain's Dream. By David Hackett Fischer

Das Kapital: A Critique of Political Economy: by Karl Marx.

Flames across the Border: 1813-1814. By Pierre Berton.

From Dictatorship to Democracy: A Conceptual Framework for Liberation: By Gene Sharp.

Hitler's Banker: Hjalmar Horace Greeley Schacht. By John Weitz..

IMMANUEL KANT Premium Collection: Complete Critiques, Philosophical Works and Essays (Including Kant's Inaugural Dissertation): Biography, The Critique ... of Ethics, Perpetual Peace and more: By Immanuel Kant and J. M. D. Meiklejohn

Justice denied: The law versus Donald Marshall: By Michael Harris

Lament for an Ocean: The Collapse of the Atlantic Cod Fishery: By Michael Harris

Lies My Teacher Told Me: Everything Your American History Textbook Got Wrong: By James W. Loewen

Neurotribes: The Legacy of Autism and the Future of Neurodiversity: By Steve Silberman.

One Flew over the Cuckoo's Nest" was written: By Ken Kesey,

On the Origin of Species: By Means of Natural Selection (Dover Thrift Editions): By Charles Darwin.

Paris 1919: Six Months That Changed the World: By Margaret MacMillan

Real Democracy in Operation; the Example of Switzerland: By Felix Bonjour.

Rules for Radicals: A Practical Primer for Realistic Radicals: By Saul D. Alinsky.

Samuel De Champlain: From New France to Cape Cod (In the Footsteps of Explorers). By Adrianna Morganelli.

Self-reliance and Other Essays. By Ralph Waldo Emerson.

Snakes in Suits: When Psychopaths Go to Work: By Paul Babiak and Robert D. Hare.

Stasi: The Untold Story of The East German Secret Police: By John O Koehler.

The Age of Uncertainty: By John Kenneth Galbraith.

The American Invasion of Canada: The War of 1812's First Year. By Pierre BertonThe Americans: By MCDOUGAL LITTLE.

The Canadian Securities Course 1993. By The Canadian Securities Institute.

The Collected Works of Rene Descartes: The Complete Works Pergamum Media (Highlights of World Literature). By Rene Descartes.

The Communist Manifesto: By Karl Marx and Friedrich Engels.

Courts from Hell - Family Injustice in Canada Paperback – Dec 27 2007. By Frank Simons

The Gulag Archipelago 1918-1956 I-II 1973. By Solzhenitsyn Aleksandr I.

The John Locke Collection, Nov 6, 2014. By John Locke.

The Naked Ape: By Desmond Morris.

The Origin of Species: By Charles Darwin.

The Peoples of Canada: A Pre-Confederation History. By J. Bumsted

The Prince: By Niccolo Machiavelli

The Power of Myth Paperback: By Joseph Campbell (Author), Bill Moyers (Author)

The Rise and fall of the Third Reich: A History of Nazi Germany. By William L. Shirer.

The Robber Barons: By Matthew Josephson.

The Second Treatise of Government and a Letter Concerning Toleration, By John Locke.

The Social Contract (Penguin Books for Philosophy). By Jean-Jacques Rousseau.

The Swiss Model – The Power of Democracy: By Venelin Tsachevsky.

The Trial of Louis Riel: Justice and Mercy Denied a Critical Legal and Political Analysis. By George R. D. Goulet

The Wealth of Nations: By Adam Smith.

Thomas Jefferson: Writings: Autobiography / Notes on the State of Virginia / Public and Private Papers / Addresses / Letters (Library of America): By Thomas Jefferson and Merrill D. Peterson.

Thomas Paine: Collected Writings: Common Sense / the Crisis / Rights of Man / the Age of Reason: By Thomas Paine.

Two Treatises of Government (Everyman). By John Locke.

Unholy Orders: Tragedy at Mount Cashel: By Michael Harris

Walden and Civil Disobedience. By Henry David Thoreau.

Without Conscience: The Disturbing World of the Psychopaths among Us: By Robert D. Hare PhD.

Cecil Rhodes and the Pursuit of Power. by Robert I. Rotberg

The Creature from Jekyll Island: A Second Look at the Federal Reserve. Jun 1 2002. by G. Edward Griffin.

Science and Human Behaviour B. F. Skinner (Author).

Beyond Freedom and Dignity (Hackett Classics) by B.F. Skinner.

Walden Two (Hackett Classics) by B. F. Skinner.

Dumbing Us Down: The Hidden Curriculum of Compulsory Schooling, by John Taylor Gatto and Zachary Slayback

by Edward Bernays and Mark Crispin Miller

Public Relations. by Edward L. Bernays

Tavistock Institute: Social engineering the Masses. by Daniel Estulin

The Open Society and Its Enemies: New One-Volume Edition. by Karl R. Popper and Alan Ryan

Man's Search for Meaning Paperback – June 1, 2006

by Viktor E. Frankl

Operation Paperclip: The Secret Intelligence. by Annie Jacobsen

The Search for the "Manchurian Candidate": The CIA and Mind Control: The Secret History of the Behavioural Sciences Paperback – by John D. Marks

Spontaneous Activity in Education (Illustrated) by Maria Montessori

The Biology of Belief 10th Anniversary Edition: Unleashing the Power of Consciousness, Matter & Miracles. by Bruce H. Lipton

The Phoenix Program. by Douglas Valentine

The Human Radiation Experiments.

by Advisory Committee on Human Radiation Experiments

Index